First World War
and Army of Occupation
War Diary
France, Belgium and Germany

55 DIVISION
166 Infantry Brigade
King's (Liverpool Regiment)
10th Battalion
30 September 1916 - 30 September 1919

WO95/2929/3

The Naval & Military Press Ltd
www.nmarchive.com
Published in association with The National Archives

Published by

The Naval & Military Press Ltd

Unit 10 Ridgewood Industrial Park,

Uckfield, East Sussex,

TN22 5QE England

Tel: +44 (0) 1825 749494

www.naval-military-press.com

www.nmarchive.com

This diary has been reprinted in facsimile from the original. Any imperfections are inevitably reproduced and the quality may fall short of modern type and cartographic standards.

© **Crown Copyright**
Images reproduced by permission of The National Archives, London, England, 2015.

Contents

Document type	Place/Title	Date From	Date To
Heading	WO95/2929/3 1/10 Bn King's Liverpool Regt. 1916 Jan-1919 Sept		
Heading	55th Division 166th Infy Bde 1-10th Bn King's Liverpool Regt Jan 1916-Sep 1919		
War Diary		00/01/1916	00/06/1916
Heading	166th Brigade 55th Division 1/10th Battalion The King's Liverpool Regiment July 1916		
Heading	War Diary Of The 1/10th Liverpool Regiment 166th Infantry Brigade 55th (West Lancashire) Division For The Period 1st July 1916 To 31st July 1916 Vol 19		
War Diary		00/07/1916	00/07/1916
Heading	166th Brigade 55th Division 1/10th Battalion The King's Liverpool Regiment August 1916		
Heading	War Diary Of The 1/10th Liverpool Regt. For The Period 1st August To 31st August 1916. Vol 20		
War Diary		00/08/1916	00/08/1916
Heading	War Diary Of 1/10th Liverpool R. 1st September To 30th September 1916 Vol 21		
War Diary	In The Field	01/10/1916	01/10/1916
Heading	War Diary Of 1/10th (Scottish) Liverpool Regt For The Period 1st To 31st October 1916 Vol 22		
War Diary	In The Field	02/11/1916	02/11/1916
Heading	War Diary Of 1/10th Liverpool Regt For Period 1st November To 30th November 1916 Vol 23		
War Diary	In The Field	01/12/1916	01/12/1916
Miscellaneous	Reference Trench Map St. Julien	29/11/1916	29/11/1916
Miscellaneous	Preliminary Report On Raid On German Trenches.	29/11/1916	29/11/1916
Heading	War Diary Of 1/10th Liverpool Regt For Period December 1st To 31st 1916 Vol 24		
War Diary	In The Field	01/01/1917	01/01/1917
Heading	War Diary Of The 1/10 Liverpool R For The Period 1/1/17 To 31/1/17 Vol 25		
War Diary	In The Field		
Heading	War Diary Of 1/10th Liverpool Regt For The Period 1st To 28th February 1917 Vol 26		
War Diary	Field	01/02/1917	01/03/1917
Heading	War Diary Of The 1/10 Liverpool Regt For The Period 1st To 31st March 1917 Vol 27		
War Diary	In The Field	01/04/1917	01/04/1917
Heading	War Diary Of 1/10 Liverpool Regt. For The Period April 1st To 30th 1917 Vol 28		
War Diary	In The Field	01/05/1917	01/05/1917
Heading	War Diary Of 1/10th Liverpool R. For The Period May 1st To 31st 1917 Vol 29		
War Diary	In The Field	01/06/1917	01/06/1917
Heading	War Diary Of 1/10 Liverpool R. For The Period June 1st To June 30th 1917 Vol 30		
War Diary	In The Field	01/07/1917	01/07/1917
Heading	War Diary Of The 1/10 Liverpool R For The Period 1st July To 31st July 1917 Vol 31		

War Diary	In The Field	01/08/1917	01/08/1917
Heading	War Diary Of 1/10th Liverpool R. For Period 1st To 31st August 1917 Vol 32		
War Diary	In The Field	31/08/1917	31/08/1917
Heading	War Diary Of 1/10th Liverpool R. For Period 1/9/17-30/9/17 Vol 33		
War Diary	In The Field	30/09/1916	30/09/1916
Heading	War Diary Of The 1/10th Liverpool R. For The Period 1st To 31st October 1917 Vol 34		
War Diary	In The Field	31/10/1917	31/10/1917
Heading	War Diary Of The 1/10th Liverpool R For The Period 1st To 30th November 1917 Vol 35		
War Diary	In The Field		
Heading	War Diary Of The 1/10th Liverpool For The Period 1st To 31st December 1917 Vol 36		
War Diary		30/11/1917	01/12/1917
Heading	War Diary Of The 1/10th Liverpool R For The Period 1st To 31st January 1918 Vol 37		
War Diary	In The Field	01/01/1918	01/01/1918
Heading	War Diary Of The 1/10th Liverpool R. For The Period 1st To 28th Febry 1918 Vol 38		
War Diary		01/02/1918	01/02/1918
Heading	War Diary Of 1/10th Liverpool R For Period 1st To 31st March 1918 Vol 39		
War Diary		00/03/1918	00/03/1918
Heading	166th Brigade 55th Division 1/10th Battalion The King's Liverpool Regiment April 1918		
War Diary	In The Field	30/04/1918	30/04/1918
Miscellaneous	'X' Coy. 1/10th Liverpool Scottish. Operations	09/04/1918	09/04/1918
Miscellaneous	Notes On Operations	09/04/1918	09/04/1918
Miscellaneous	9 Platoon 'Y' Company	09/04/1918	09/04/1918
Miscellaneous	Experience Of 10 Platoon	09/04/1918	09/04/1918
Miscellaneous	Y Coy 12 Platoon	01/08/1918	01/08/1918
Miscellaneous	Narrative Of Operations Of 'Y' Company	09/04/1918	09/04/1918
Miscellaneous	Happenings	09/04/1918	09/04/1918
Miscellaneous	April 9th To 16th		
Miscellaneous	Narrative Of Tour In The Line	09/04/1918	09/04/1918
Miscellaneous	Mesplaux Farm To Raimbert	09/04/1918	09/04/1918
Miscellaneous	Report On Counter Attack	14/04/1918	14/04/1918
Miscellaneous	1/10th (Scottish) Battn. The King's (L'Pool Regiment)	18/04/1918	18/04/1918
Miscellaneous	Narrative Of Operations	03/08/1918	03/08/1918
Miscellaneous	Narrative Of Operations	13/04/1918	13/04/1918
Heading	War Diary Of 10th Liverpool R For Period 1st To 31st May 1918 Vol 41		
War Diary	In The Field	31/05/1918	31/05/1918
Heading	War Diary Of 10th Liverpool R For Period 1st To 30th June 1918 Vol 42		
War Diary		01/06/1918	31/07/1918
Heading	War Diary Of 10th Lpool R For Period 1st To 31st August 1918 Vol 44		
War Diary		01/08/1918	31/08/1918
Heading	War Diary Of 10th Liverpool R For Period 1st To 30th September 1918 Vol 45		
War Diary		01/09/1918	30/09/1918
Heading	War Diary Of 10th Liverpool R For Period 1st To 31st October 1918 Vol 46		

War Diary		01/10/1918	31/10/1918
Heading	War Diary Of 10th Bn Liverpool R for the Period 1st-30th November 1918 Vol 47		
War Diary	Esplechin	01/11/1918	04/11/1918
War Diary	Froidmont	05/11/1918	07/11/1918
War Diary	Ere	08/11/1918	25/11/1918
War Diary	Ath	26/11/1918	30/11/1918
Heading	War Diary Of 10th Liverpool R For Period 1st To 31st December 1918 Vol 48		
War Diary		01/12/1918	31/01/1919
Miscellaneous	Report On Battalion Educational Scheme	01/02/1919	01/02/1919
Heading	War Diary 10th Liverpool R February 1919 Vol 50		
War Diary		01/02/1919	28/02/1919
Heading	War Diary For 1/10 Bn Liverpool Scottish Antwerp For June 1919		
War Diary		01/06/1919	30/06/1919
Miscellaneous	Herewith War Diary For The Month Of July	31/07/1919	31/07/1919
War Diary		01/07/1919	31/07/1919
Heading	O.C. 10th Bn. Kings Liverpool Regt Aug 1919		
War Diary		01/08/1919	31/08/1919
Miscellaneous	Herewith War Diary For The Month Of September 1919	30/09/1919	30/09/1919
War Diary		01/09/1919	30/09/1919

WO 95 2929/3

1/10 Bn King's Liverpool Regt.
1916 Jan – 1919 Sept

55TH DIVISION
166TH INFY BDE

1-10TH BN KING'S LIVERPOOL REGT
JAN 1916-SEP 1919

FROM 3DIV 9BDE

55TH DIVISION
166TH INFY BDE

WAR DIARY
INTELLIGENCE SUMMARY

10th (SCOTTISH) BN. THE KING'S (L'POOL REGT.)

Hour, Date, Place	Summary of Events and Information	Remarks and references to Appendices
JANUARY 1916	New Year's Day, when the Battn was resting in the Camp at RENINGHELST was given to the men as a general holiday, except for one parade, when the Commanding Officer presented the gifts from the wives & relations of the Officers of the Battalion. Orders were received the same day that the Battn was to be transferred from the 9th Brigade 3rd Divn to the 166th Brigade, 55th Divn. The Battn was inspected on the 4th by the G.O.C. 9th Infy Brigade (Brig Gen W Douglas Smith), who, in a farewell address expressed his regret at losing the (Newport portion) from his Command. For over a year, the Battn had been foremost in all the Brigade had done, both in fighting the games & in the future he would miss the Battn very much. Two days later, the G.O.C. III Divn (Major Gen A Haldane) in inspecting the Battn wished all ranks Godspeed & Good luck, and thanked them for all they had done. The move to the new area commenced on the morning of the 8th. The III Divn Band accompanied the Battn part of the way to BAILLEUL, where entrainment took place under passed orders. Orders were to report to the R.T.O. at PONT REMY, after detraining there, the Battn marches via AIRAINES to HUECOURT arriving at 11pm on the 9th a very fine performance	132

WAR DIARY
INTELLIGENCE SUMMARY
(Erase heading not required.)

Army Form C. 2118.

Hour, Date, Place	Summary of Events and Information	Remarks and references to Appendices
JANUARY 1916	Later in the day, the 2 O C 166" Infantry Brigade (Brig Gen J. Green Wilkinson) visited the C.O to welcome the Battn on joining his Brigade. A Draft of 83 other Ranks arrived from ENGLAND on the 10th. For the remainder of the month, the Battn carried out training at HEUCOURT. Parade grounds were erected & rifle ranges built. The programme of training included Physical Drill Bayonet Fighting Section, Platoon & Company Drill, Musketry, Range Practice & Visual Training, Route Marching & Trench Stripping. Inter Company Shooting matches were held. Sports & Recreation for the men were not neglected, A Sports Committee being chosen & football matches & paper chases announced. A Regimental Wet Canteen was opened. On the 29th the 55th Divn was inspected by Lt Gen XIV Corps (The Earl of Cavan) at HALLENCOURT, on which occasion the Battn paraded with a strength of 22 officers & 393 other Ranks. During the month the following Officers arrived 2nd Lts. (A. N. Berrork, F. C. HULME, J W G POCKETT, N E SWINDELLS. Wasmelter M.D.	

Army Form C. 2118.

WAR DIARY
or
INTELLIGENCE SUMMARY.

(Erase heading not required.)

Instructions regarding War Diaries and Intelligence Summaries are contained in F. S. Regs., Part II. and the Staff Manual respectively. Title pages will be prepared in manuscript.

Place	Date	Hour	Summary of Events and Information	Remarks and references to Appendices
	AUGUST 1919.			
	28th.		Three trains arrived. Weather dull but warm. Battalion Team beat "Z" Coy. at football by 10 goals to nil.	
	29th.		No trains. Weather dull with showers.	
	30th.		Three trains arrived from Cavalry Division. Weather dull with showers.	
	31st.		Three trains arrived. Weather cool and bright. No. demobilized during the month :- 2 Officers, 10 other ranks. No. demobilized to date :- 35 Officers 664 other ranks.	

J.A. ????

Lieut. Colonel.
Commanding 10th Bn. The King's (Liverpool Regiment)(Liverpool Scottish).

BASE CAMP,
ANTWERP.
August 31st 1919.

To:- Camp Commandant.
      Embarkation Camp.
      Antwerp.

Reference B.R.O. 275 dated 5.7.19.

Herewith War Diary for the month of SEPTEMBER 1919 for disposal in accordance with instructions contained therein.

                                              Lieut.Col.
                     Commanding LIVERPOOL SCOTTISH.

Base Camp, ANtwerp.
  September 30th 1919.

Army Form C. 2118.

WAR DIARY
or
INTELLIGENCE SUMMARY.
(Erase heading not required.)

Instructions regarding War Diaries and Intelligence Summaries are contained in F. S. Regs., Part II. and the Staff Manual respectively. Title pages will be prepared in manuscript.

Place	Date	Hour	Summary of Events and Information	Remarks and references to Appendices
SEPTEMBER 1919	1st.		Battalion still encamped at Bassin Dock, Antwerp, the same administrative work in connection with the Embarkation Camp being carried out.	
	2nd.		Return of fine weather. 2/Lt.Heggie demobilized Demobilization of July 1st Derby Men commenced.	
	3rd.		Weather fine and warm. No trains. 2/Lt.F.McDonald returns from tour of Battlefields.	
	4th		Weather fine. No trains. Concert Party give a Good Show.	
	5th		Weather fine. No trains arrived. Boxing Contest advertised at 14.30 hours 6th cancelled. - Tournament commences at 17.00 hours in No.1 Dining Hall.	
	6th		Weather fine. No trains.	
			Weather fine and warm. No trains. Boxing Tournament held in Camp, very good attendance. Parker beat Leroi (Belgian Heavyweight) McCabthy won Semi-Final but was unable to fight in final. McDonald beat Whittington.	
	7th		Weather continues fine. 3 Trains arrived. Church Parade.	

Army Form C. 2118.

WAR DIARY
or
INTELLIGENCE SUMMARY.

(Erase heading not required.)

Instructions regarding War Diaries and Intelligence Summaries are contained in F. S. Regs., Part II. and the Staff Manual respectively. Title pages will be prepared in manuscript.

Place	Date	Hour	Summary of Events and Information	Remarks and references to Appendices
SEPTEMBER 1919.	8th		Weather good. No Trains. Concert Party proceed to Cologne. 140 Other Ranks proceed for Dispersal. 2/Lt.C.S.Patterson Demobbed. 2/Lt.F.McDonald do.	
	9th		Weather good. No trains.	
	10th		Weather fine. One train arrived. Instructions issued for the Riband of the Victory Medal to be worn.	
	11th		Weather showery. Two trains arrived.	
	12th		Weather fine. No trains.	
	13th		Weather fine. No trains. Scrubbing etc' of Huts. Report of Concert Party in "Cologne Post".	
	14th		Weather dull and warm. No trains. Church Parades. Football Team played at CAPPELLIN -- XXXWXXXXX Draw 2 -2 after a good game. This is the first match the Team has failed to win. Tea was provided for the Team.	
	15th			

Army Form C. 2118.

WAR DIARY
or
INTELLIGENCE SUMMARY.
(Erase heading not required.)

Instructions regarding War Diaries and Intelligence Summaries are contained in F. S. Regs, Part II. and the Staff Manual respectively. Title pages will be prepared in manuscript.

Place	Date	Hour	Summary of Events and Information	Remarks and references to Appendices
SEPTEMBER 1919.	15th		Weather fine. No trains. Bathing plentiful in the Moat.	
	16th		No trains. Weather fair.	
	17th		Weather fine. Instructions given out as to the wearing of the Medal Ribands. No trains. Lt. Cream returns from leave to United Kingdom.	
	18th		Weather good. No trains. G.O.C. - in - CHIEF expected to visit the Camp on Friday - all available men to be ready for Muster Parade.	
	19th		Weather good - dull. No trains arrived. G.O.C. - in - CHIEF did not arrive as expected.	
	20th		Weather dull. Scrubbing of Huts etc., G.O.C. - in - CHIEF arrived at Camp about eleven o'clock in the morning. No Muster Parade or Guard of Honour.	
	21st		Weather bad - rain - cold. Swimming Gala had to be postponed owing to low temperature of water and bad weather.	
	22nd		Weather showery. No trains arrived.	

Army Form C. 2118.

WAR DIARY
or
INTELLIGENCE SUMMARY.

(Erase heading not required.)

Instructions regarding War Diaries and Intelligence Summaries are contained in F. S. Regs., Part II. and the Staff Manual respectively. Title pages will be prepared in manuscript.

Place	Date	Hour	Summary of Events and Information	Remarks and references to Appendices
SEPTEMBER 1919.				
	23rd		Weather showery. No trains.	
	24th		Weather dull. One train arrived.	
	25th		Weather cold and stormy. One train arrived.	
	26th		Lt.Col Munro. left for Cologne. Weather cool. No trains.	
	27th		Weather dull. No trains.	
	28th		Weather dull and showery. No trains. Battalion Team beat No.6 Stationary Hospital at Football.10 - Nil.	
	29th		Weather fine. No trains.	
	30th		Weather fine. No trains. Lt.Col.Munro returns from Cologne.	

NO. DEMOBILIZED DURING MONTH OF SEPTEMBER 3 Officers & 150 O.R
NO. DEMOBILIZED TO DATE.   38 Officers & 812 Other Ranks.

Embarkation Camp, ANTWERP.
30th September 1919.

J.O.Munro   Lt.Col.
Commanding LIVERPOOL SCOTTISH.

Army Form C. 2118.

WAR DIARY
or
INTELLIGENCE SUMMARY.

(Erase heading not required.)

Instructions regarding War Diaries and Intelligence Summaries are contained in F.S. Regs., Part II. and the Staff Manual respectively. Title pages will be prepared in manuscript.

Place	Date	Hour	Summary of Events and Information	Remarks and references to Appendices
	AUGUST 1919.			
	18th.		Weather continues warm. No trains arrived. Bellingham. A Lecture was given in the Camp Cinema by Mr. Billington on "Camera and Caravan" which was appreciated by all who attended.	
	19th.		Weather very warm. No trains arrived. Another very interesting Lecture was given by Mr. Billington [Bellingham] the subject being "The Rise and Fall of Spain". 2/Lt. W. B. James reported for duty with the Battalion from the 25th Bn. The King's Liverpool Regt.	
	20th.		Weather warm. No trains but the usual Camp Fatigues &c.	
	21st.		Weather cooler. Three trains arrived. A Football Match against the 60th Labour Coy. resulted in a win for the Battalion by 5 goals to 3.	
	22nd.		Weather cool and fine. Three trains arrived. Outbreak of Fire at 54 Hangar on the Docks, but nothing serious.	
	23rd.		Fire Alarm sounded shortly after mid-night, the cause of same being a Motor Lorry on fire at the R.A.S.C. park, but same was soon extinguished. First fall of rain for many weeks. Three trains arrived.	
	24th.		Weather showery. No trains arrived.	
	25th.		Weather bright. 3 trains arrived.	
	26th.		Weather showery. 3 trains arrived, including a Guard from the 52nd Leicester Regt. lately attached to us for duty.	
	27th.		Weather stormy. 3 trains arrived.	

Army Form C. 2118.

WAR DIARY
or
INTELLIGENCE SUMMARY.
(Erase heading not required.)

Instructions regarding War Diaries and Intelligence Summaries are contained in F.S. Regs., Part II. and the Staff Manual respectively. Title pages will be prepared in manuscript.

Place	Date	Hour	Summary of Events and Information	Remarks and references to Appendices
	AUGUST 1919.			
	10th.		Glorious weather continues. Four trains arrived. Battalion Team played EDEGEM at Football and won by four goals to one after a strenuous game. Tea was provided and a very enjoyable afternoon was spent.	
	11th.		Weather very hot. Bathing plentiful in the Moat. 16 Cadres arrived.	
	12th.		Weather very warm. One train arrived.	
	13th.		Weather very warm. Detachment of 200 of the Royal Fusiliers arrived to relieve the Detachment of the Leicester Regt.	
	14th.		Weather continued very hot. Four trains arrived. The Battalion Officers beat the Brigade Officers at Football by 2 goals. The Battalion Team beat the Leicesters at Football by 2 goals to 1 in the farewell match. Capt. R.T. Ainsworth returned from leave.	
	15th.		Continuation of the warm weather. Four trains arrived.	
	16th.		Weather very warm. Four trains arrived. A Concert was given by "D" Coy. of the Royal Fusiliers in the Camp Cinema.	
	17th.		Weather very warm. Sports held at Lierre. The Battalion sent a party of competitors who returned to Camp without taking part owing to the unsportsman-like attitude of the Belgian judges. A good day spoiled. Capt. A.M. McGilchrist demobilized. Detachment of the Leicester Regt. returned to Germany to join their Battalion. Three trains arrived.	

LIVERPOOL SCOTTISH.

WAR DIARY or INTELLIGENCE SUMMARY.

Army Form C. 2118.

(Erase heading not required.)

Place	Date	Hour	Summary of Events and Information	Remarks and references to Appendices
	AUGUST 1919.			
	1st.		The Battalion still encamped at BASSIN DOCK, ANTWERP, carrying out the same administrative work in connection with the EMBARKATION CAMP. Weather cool. No trains.	
	2nd.		Weather fine. One train arrived.	
	3rd.		Weather cool. One train arrived.	
	4th.		(Bank Holiday) General Holiday. Weather warm and fine. One train. The Battalion defeated the 60th Labour Coy. at Football after a good game by 7 goals to 0.	
	5th.		No trains arrived. Weather warm.	
	6th.		Major. Hart of the 52nd Bn. Leicester Regt. left this Station to take over Command of the Notts and Derby Regt. on the Rhine. Lt.Col.Munro, DSO,MC,DCM, returned from leave to U.K. and resumed command of the Battalion. Major. R.H.D.Lockhart TD, proceeded on leave to U.K. No trains arrived. Weather fine.	
	7th.		One train arrived. Usual Camp fatigues &c. Weather fine and warm	
	8th.		Weather continues fine and warm. No trains.	
	9th.		Battalion Sports Day. Sports were held in glorious weather and largely attended by all ranks and visitors to the Camp. The prizes were presented to the successful competitors by Lt.Col. Munro, DSO, MC,DCM. who thanked the Committee for their efforts. "Z" Coy. won the Battalion Inter-Company Shield. Everybody voted the Sports a huge success. Four trains arrived with Equipment Guards, from the Highland Divn.	

O.C. 10th Bn. King's Liverpool
Regt.

Aug. 1919.

Army Form C. 2118.

WAR DIARY
or
INTELLIGENCE SUMMARY.
(Erase heading not required.)

Instructions regarding War Diaries and Intelligence Summaries are contained in F. S. Regs., Part II. and the Staff Manual respectively. Title pages will be prepared in manuscript.

Place	Date	Hour	Summary of Events and Information	Remarks and references to Appendices
	JULY 1919			
	25th		9 Equipment Guards arrived. Weather Changeable. British Dance in connection with Peace Celebrations. -- very successful	
	26th		Saturday. 9 Cadres, weather still unsettled 30 Other Ranks and Pipe Band took part in Torchlight Procession in Antwerp.	
	27th		Sunday. Weather, still raining --- 9 Cadres arrived 2/Lieut C.LYON reported for Duty from 13th Bn King's (Liverpool Regiment)	
	28th		Weather cool and showery ---- No Trains arrived. Fatigue parties clearing debris of Fire from Hangar No. 52.	
	29th		Weather chilly ---- No Trains arrived. Demobbed to date 33 Officers and 651 Other Ranks.	
	30th		Weather fine and bright. No trains.	
	31st		Weather cool ----- No trains. No. demobilized during Month 10 Other Ranks. No. demobilized to date 33 Officers and 658 Other Ranks.	
BASE CAMP ANTWERP	July 31st 1919.			

R.M.Lockhart. Major.
Commanding 10th Battn "The King's"(Liverpool Regiment) (Liverpool Scottish)

Army Form C. 2118.

WAR DIARY
or
INTELLIGENCE SUMMARY.
(Erase heading not required.)

Instructions regarding War Diaries and Intelligence Summaries are contained in F.S. Regs., Part II. and the Staff Manual respectively. Title pages will be prepared in manuscript.

Place	Date	Hour	Summary of Events and Information	Remarks and references to Appendices
	JULY			
	19th		Saturday - Day of British Peace Celebrations, observed as a General Holiday throughout the Army. Camp was roused about 4.0 a.m. by a fire breaking out at Camp Q.M. & Ration Stores, considerable damage was done but the Fire was prevented from damaging the Church Army Hut. C.S.M.Donaldson was highly complimented on the iniative and energy which he displayed. The fire was well under Control when the ANTWERP FIRE BRIGADE arrived. In the afternoon Sports were held in Camp there was a large attendance and some very interesting Events took place. There was a heavy thunder storm during the interval for Tea, in consequence of which the continuation of the Sports in the evening was postponed to a later date. Lieuts. J.E.COOKSON and C.A.WHITE appointed A/Captains.	
	20th		Sunday - Plenty of rain. 6 Other Ranks took part in Swimming Gala organized by the Antwerp Swimming Club, 4 of them won prizes	
	21st		Belgian National Fete. 100 Liverpool Scottish and 100 Leicesters and Pipe Band took part in procession in Antwerp. As usual they were warmly appreciated	
	22nd		First train for 12 days - 7 Equipment Guards arrived Weather very wet	
	23rd		Weather cool and showery 7 Cadres arrived Demobilized todate - 33 Officers 648 O/R's	
	24th		More rain 7 Cadres arrived Fire alarm was sounded at 15.00 hours for small outbreak of Fire near Transport Lines	

Army Form C. 2118.

WAR DIARY
or
INTELLIGENCE SUMMARY.
(Erase heading not required.)

Instructions regarding War Diaries and Intelligence Summaries are contained in F. S. Regs., Part II. and the Staff Manual respectively. Title pages will be prepared in manuscript.

Place	Date	Hour	Summary of Events and Information	Remarks and references to Appendices
	JULY 9th		Rainy Weather Tennis Courts (Hard) being made in the Camp - 1 for Officers and 1 for Men	
	10th		Showery weather Remainder of the 55th Division arrived as Equipment Guards.	
	11th		Showery but Warm No trains today but large fatigue parties removing debris of Fire at Hangar 52. Demobilized todate 30 Officers and 647 Other Ranks	
	12th		Saturday - Showery Played 52nd Leicesters SOCCER and won 4-0 after a very good game	
	13th		Sunday - No trains Pipe Band played in a Torchlight Procession at ANTWERP in honour of French Fete.	
	14th		Still no trains, plenty of rain 200 all ranks and Pipe Band took part in French National Fete, great reception	
	15th		Weather changeable - No trains	
	16th		Weather still unsettled No trains, large fatigues parties still employed on removing Fire Debris from Hangar 52. 2/Lieut J.B.McKAY (10th A & S. Hdrs) to be T/Lt vide "London Gazette"	
	17th		Weather fine and warm No Cinema Show given	
	18th		Weather very warm - No trains arrived, fatigue parties still working at Hangar 52	

Army Form C. 2118.

WAR DIARY
or
INTELLIGENCE SUMMARY.
(Erase heading not required.)

Instructions regarding War Diaries and Intelligence Summaries are contained in F.S. Regs., Part II. and the Staff Manual respectively. Title pages will be prepared in manuscript.

Place	Date	Hour	Summary of Events and Information	Remarks and references to Appendices
	JULY 6th		Weather fine, brilliant Sunshine. The remains of the late Capt. C.A.Fryatt were brought from Bruges to Antwerp for Embarkation on a British Destroyer. The Guards of Honour included 100 Other Ranks of this Battalion with Pipe and Brass Bands under Command of Capt.A.M.McGILCHRIST assisted by Lieut. R.McD.B.MACDONALD and 2/Lieut. F.McDONALD also Lieut. S.M.O.TALLIS and 25 Other Ranks of the 52nd Leicesters, attached to this Battalion for Duty. The Pall Bearers were 8 Sergeants of this Unit under Lieut.A.McR.CRAM. A Choir of 50 Other Ranks of the LIVERPOOL SCOTTISH and 50 Other Ranks of the LEICESTERS under 2/Lieut. C.S.PATTERSON. were formed up on the STEEN. A religious Service was held on the STEEN before the Coffin was transferred to H.M.S. "ORPHEUS". The procession through the streets from Gare Centrale, Avenue Du Keyser, Place De Meir, STEEN was a most impressive one and the Battalion was complimented on its splendid turnout.	
	7th		Weather fine sunshine throughout the day. The following cadres arrived:- 15th Division H.Q. R.A. & R.E. 275th Bde H.Q. (R.F.A.) 46th Brigade H.Q. " " Sig. Sub Section 15th Division Signal Coy A/276 " F.A. A/275 Bde R.F.A. 439 Field Coy R.E. B/275 Bde R.F.A A/117th Bde R.F.A C/275 Bde do. B/117th " " D/275 Bde do 800 Other Ranks proceeded to BOULOGNE from this Camp en Route to England for Demobilization	
	8th		Major Hart (Leicesters) left for Cologne to take charge of Company in Victory March in PARIS Football Match versus 52nd Leicesters resulted in a win for the SCOTTISH 3-1. after a splendid game	

Army Form C. 2118.

WAR DIARY
or
INTELLIGENCE SUMMARY.
(Erase heading not required.)

Instructions regarding War Diaries and Intelligence Summaries are contained in F. S. Regs., Part II and the Staff Manual respectively. Title pages will be prepared in manuscript.

Place	Date	Hour	Summary of Events and Information	Remarks and references to Appendices
	JULY 1919			
	1st		Battalion still encamped at BASSIN DOCK, ANTWERP, the same administrative work IN CONNECTION WITH THE Embarkation Camp being carried out Wet weather 3 Legged Race won by "D" Coy Advised of the return to Rhine of the Sherwood Foresters attached to us, they have been splendid workers and good fellows all round and we shall be sorry to loose them. The 52nd Leicesters are relieving them	
	2nd		Weather showery Lieut. McCLYMONT took over Command of "D" COY vice 2/Lieut MACDONALD. Education Classes going fairly well	

	3rd		Weather changeable occasional showers
			The 52nd Leicesters arrived to relieve the Sherwood Foresters, 6 Officers and 200 Other Ranks:-
			    Major. L.H.P.Hart
			    Capt.R.L.Hett
			    Lieut.B.A.Taylor
			      " S.W.G.Tallis
			    2/Lieut S.Clancy
			      " M.W.Marratt	

	4th		Dull morning, heavy rain in afternoon American Independence Day, there were celebrations in ANTWERP and the Battalion was represented, in a procession by the Pipe Band, 25 Other Ranks, LIVERPOOL SCOTTISH, 25 Other Ranks 52nd LEICESTERS, under Capt.R.T.AINSWORTH. Several speeches were given at the "Knights of Columbus" the (American Club) Several American Bands were stationed in Antwerp for the occasion and great excitement prevailed in the Streets during the Evening	
	5th		Weather fine and very hot during the day	

F.R/1088

To:-

Camp ~~Commandant~~
Embarkation Camp
Antwerp

Reference B.R.O. 275 Dated 5th July 1919.

Herewith War Diary for the Month of July for disposal in accordance with instructions contained therein.

R.A.D Lockhart.
Major
Commanding LIVERPOOL SCOTTISH

Base Camp, Antwerp
July 31st 1919.

Base. H.Q.

Forwarded.

Lieut. Col.
Cmdg. Embarkation Camp.

WAR DIARY or INTELLIGENCE SUMMARY

Sheet 5.

Place	Date	Hour	Summary of Events and Information
JUNE 1919.	25th (Continued)		1/3rd W.L. Fld. Amb. 419th Fld.Co. R.E. 36th Bn.L.S. C.H.Q. & 2 Coys. 10th East Kents. 15th Suff.Regt. 15th R.Suss.Regt. 341 Co. R.A.S.C. 543 Co. R.A.S.C. 543rd Co. R.A.S.C. 544th Co. R.A.S.C. No.2 Traff.Con.Squad
	26th		Beautiful weather. Funeral of Private Ingram at ZWAANDE. Pipers, Firing Party and 'D' Company attended. Beautiful wreathes were sent by the Officers and Men. 5-a-Side Football Competition - 1st Company beat 'D' Coy 2-0.
	27th		Rain during the Day. Obstacle Race of 2 miles was won by C.Q.M.S. Montgomery.
	28th		Fine and Breezy. Sergeants' Race was won by C.Q.M.S. Thomas. News of the Draft of 140 Other Ranks on their way from BOULOGNE. Signing of the Peace Treaty was gladly received by all Ranks.
	29th		Weather - Showery. Draft of 140 O/Rs. arrived - several old members of the Battalion received a warm reception. 600 Other Ranks proceeded from Camp to BOULOGNE on their way to England for Demobilization.
	30th		Weather - Dull but fine. Day passed quietly. B'tln.Team beat 169 Bde.R.F.A. Cairo - Capt.Mean won 9-1.
			No. DEMOBILIZED DURING MONTH OF JUNE... 4 Officers & 7 Other Ranks. No. DEMOBILIZED TO DATE................. 33 Officers & 644 Other Ranks.
Embarkation Camp, ANTWERP. 30th June 1919.			R.W.Strathland Major. Commanding LIVERPOOL SCOTTISH.

WAR DIARY
or
INTELLIGENCE SUMMARY.
(Erase heading not required.)

Place	Date	Hour	Summary of Events and Information
June 1919.	20th.		Tug-o'-War&a Final. Transport won. Putting the Weight. "Z" Coy. won. with a 29½ ft "PUT".
	21st.		A little rain fell during the night, rained during afternoon. 55th Divnl Cadres starting to come through. DAQ arrived. The following Cadres also arrived to-day:- 47th Bde Sig.Sub.Sec. 2nd Div. S.S.Co. D/71st Bde RHA. 71st Bde RFA HQ. 71st Bde Sig. Sub. 9th Gordon Hdrs (Pnrs). 40 Fld.Amb. 5th DAC. (1st and 2nd Sec.) 400th 3rd&4th RFA. 410th 3rd&4th RFA.
	22nd.		Fine and a good breeze. Captain and Adjt. T.E.Roddick demobilized via Ostend.
	23rd.		Rain and Cold. Lt.C.A.White takes over the duties of Adjutant.vice Roddick Demob. The following Cadres arrived today:- D/153th AFA. 158th AF.Bde HQ. 46th Fld.Amb. 55th An. MCC.(HQ & 1st Coy) B/153rd Bde. C/153 Bde. D/153 Bde. 14th A.&.S.Hdrs. 10th HLI. 29th HLI.
	24th.		165th Brigade Cadres are arriving in the Camp. - Quite a number of old friends. Col Munro leaves to U.K. The following Cadres arrived today:- 9th Seaforth Hdrs. 5thCamerons. 42th Inf.Bde HQ. 47th Fld.Amb. 1/4th K.L.Regt 2/5th Lcnos.Fus. 1/4th L.N.L. 15th R.L.I.Rgt. 9th R.L.Irish Rgt. 9th KOYLI Fus. 14th Co. 1 Hars. 13th Som.L.I. 13th Devon.Regt. 2nd Cav.Div.HQ. 2nd Cav.Div.V.HC (ALSC) 5th H.T.Co. 146th Mob.Vet.Sec.
	25th.		Very wet day. Visited St Nicholas and had a Civic Reception in the Town Hall afterwards played the local Team football, and won 8-0. 358116 Pte Lathan W. died very suddenly. The following Cadres arrived today. 7/8th K.O.S.B. 9th R.S. 74th Fld.Co.RE. 27th N.V.S. 154th Inf.Bde. 1/5 Toot R

WAR DIARY
or
INTELLIGENCE SUMMARY.
(Erase heading not required.)

Place	Date	Hour	Summary of Events and Information
June 1919.	14th.		A lovely day. Leeds Ashwell's Party gave "Caroline" in the Camp Theatre. Transport won the final of the Tug-of-War. The following Cadres arrived today:- 70th Bde.R.F.A. H.Q. B/Batty 70th Bde.RFA. C/Batty 70th Bde.RFA. D/Batty 70th Bde.RFA. Sig. Sub.Sec.R.F.A.
	15th.		We played Tankize today. Won 3-0. Magnificent welcome. Procession of Political Parties. Beautiful day. The following Cadre arrived today......8th D.A.C.
	16th.		Anniversary of Hooge 1915. Captain Roddick and Capt.McGilchrist proceeded to the scenes of our fighting to put better crosses on the graves of members of the Battalion. First train departed for Boulogne with Cadres.
	17th.		Fine weather. Col. Munro proceeded on leave in afternoon, wired to return in the evening, owing to the situation in GERMANY. The HUNS may not sign the TREATY. The following Cadres arrived today. 1st Div. Sig. Corps. 8th Div. H.Q. H.Q.R.A.R.E. Emp.Coy. 1/7th DLI (Pioneers) 1/5th Mob. Vet.Sec. 15th DAC.(Nos. 1 & 2 Secs.less 7 GS wagons) 15th North.Lancs. 47th Bde RFA. (HQ) 47th Bde.Sig.Sub.Sec. A/47 Bde RFA 52nd Field Co.RE. 23rd London Regt. 8th Wilts.Regt. (Wilts.Yeo.)
	18th.		Still terribly hot weather. Throwing Cricket Ball Competition 1st, 2nd, "Z" Coy. 3rd. Winner threw 105 yds. The following Cadres arrived today:- A/119th AFA Bde.-B/119th AFA Bde.-C/119th AFA Bde.-15th Div. HQ.-S.A.L.No.1.Sec. B/47 Bde RFA. C/47 Bde RFA. D/47 Bde RFA.-550th Fd Co.RE.-15th Yks & Lanc. Regt. and 15th Manchester Regiment.
	19th.		Very hot today. Offrs Mess v Sergeants versus Batt.n.Recrn. Battn. Team won 6-0. STILL unbeaten.

Sheet 2.

WAR DIARY
or
INTELLIGENCE SUMMARY.
(Erase heading not required).

Instructions regarding War Diaries and Intelligence Summaries are contained in F.S. Regs., Part II. and the Staff Manual respectively. Title pages will be prepared in manuscript.

Place	Date	Hour	Summary of Events and Information
MUHR 1919.	5th Contd.		The following Cadres arrived today:- B/48 Batty. RFA. C/48 Batty RFA. D/45 Batty RFA. 1 Coy & HQ-24 MHG 74th Field Ambulance.
	6th.		Played RFA Cadre Football. won 5-2. Holiday for King's Birthday instead of 3rd instant.
	7th.		~~Whit Sunday~~ Played RFA Cadre. won 7-2.
	8th.		S.S. "Arbroath" sailed also "Kalix" with Transport. Very good send-off. 1000 men aboard Hot weather. WHIT MONDAY.
	9th.		A General Holiday. Our football team played LIERRE and won 1-0. A very good game and a very good reception.
	10th.		Lena Ashwell's Concert Party gave "Cousin Kate". A splendid performance in the Camp Cinema. The following Cadres arrived today:- H.Q. 33rd Bde RFA. HQ 33rd Bde Sgnl Sub.Sec. 32nd Batty RFA. 33rd Batty RFA. 56th Batty RFA.
	11th.		S.S. "Sicilian" (makes an extra trip) also Kalix and two barges. Captain R. Johnson who has been in France ever since the Battn. came out. Nov 1.1914 was demobilized today, and sailed on the "Sicilian". He was the last to leave of those who had been out the whole time. A splendid record. Lt.L. Cooper takes over duty as Transport Officer to the Battalion. The following Cadres arrived today: 55th Batty RFA. 45th Bde RFA HQ. 45th Bde RFA Sig.Sub.Sec. 1st Btty RFA 3rd Batty RFA.
	12th.120 Other		Ranks have left England to join us at Antwerp. s.s. "Arbroath" and "Huntsolyde" have arrived. The following Cadres arrived today. 5th Batty RFA. 57th Batty RFA. 2nd Rifle Bde.
	13th.Gusty Weather.		s.s. "Arbroath" sailed today, also the "Huntsolyde" taking 800 troops. Remainder of Cadres will go by train to Boulogne, and cross from there. No more boats are available for men. No arrivals today.

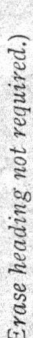

WAR DIARY
or
INTELLIGENCE SUMMARY.
(Erase heading not required.)

Instructions regarding War Diaries and Intelligence Summaries are contained in F. S. Regs., Part II. and the Staff Manual respectively. Title pages will be prepared in manuscript.

ORDERLY ROOM
LIVERPOOL SCOTTISH

Place	Date	Hour	Summary of Events and Information
JUNE 1919.	1st.		Battalion still encamped at Bassin Dock, ANTWERP, the same administrative work in connection with the Embarkation Camp being carried out.
			Very fine weather.
			The following Cadres arrived today.
			50th M.T. Co. R.A.S.C.
			(No.7 A.A.H.R.)
	2nd.		Cool Day.
			The fire-alarm was sounded at 0500 hours. A HUT (wood) full of clothing and feet, caught fire and was burnt to the ground. Our Ordnance Stores were in danger, but the local fire-brigade put out the small outbreak on the roof. Our Camp Fire Staff did very good work. The only Government Property damaged are a number of tent-boards.
			The following Cadres arrived today:-
			Nil.
	3rd.		The King's Birthday.
			The following Cadres arrived today.
			14 M.B. 56 Fld Coy. R.E. 1/7th Bn Cheshire Regt. 114 I.B. (R.H.A.)
			2nd Cyclist Bn. 1st. Yorks. A/58 Batty. RFA. 8th Royal West Kents.
			77th Fld Amb. 1st. North. Staffs. 9th R.Suss. Regt. 7th Gordon Regt.
	4th.		Weather Cool.
			Right H.lf Battn. Played Left Half Bn. A good game ending a draw 2 - 2.
			A concert at night was given by our Battn. Concert Party "The Jocks".
			The following Cadres arrived to-day.
			7th North-d Regt. 3rd Coy. 24th Bn. L.G.C. 73rd Fiel.d Amb. 48th Bde RFA H.Q.
			A/48 Batty RFA A/36 Batty R.F.A. 155th Bde R.F.A. HQ. U Batty RHA.
			T. Batty RHA. 5th Field Coy. RE.
	5th.		Education Classes started again. Classes in English, French, Mathematics, Shorthand are commencing tomorrow 6/6/19.
			S.S. Widdle sails with a thousand men on her last journey with Cadres. She goes on to Archangel (Russian Relief Force) Service. (For Cadr's see-2)
			contd.

WAR DIARY

for

1/10 Bn. LIVERPOOL SCOTTISH, Antwerp.

for

JUNE 1919.

WAR DIARY
LIVERPOOL SCOTTISH
INTELLIGENCE SUMMARY.

(Erase heading not required.)

Army Form C. 2118.

Place	Date	Hour	Summary of Events and Information	Remarks and references to Appendices
	1919. February.			
	23rd.		Sunday. Voluntary Church Parade. Final Divl. Rugby Competition resulted as follows:- 419 Field Coy.R.E's 19 points. 1/4th K.O.R.L. NIL.	
	24th.		Coy. Training. Replay against the 1/6th Bn. Cam. Hdrs. resulted in a further draw of 2 goals each. The match was played on the Cameron ground, BRAIN le COMTE.	
	25th.		Coy. training.	
	26th.		Advance party consisting of Lieuts. ROBERTS & AITKEN and 50 O/Ranks proceeded to ANTWERP to prepare hutments for the Battn. It is understood that the Battn. will form part of the Base Staff at ANTWERP to demobilise the Cadres of B.E.F. Units. The C.O. (Major LOCKHART) inspected the Battn. by Coys.	
	27th.		The Brigadier inspected the Battn. in walking out dress in the morning. In further replay, the Battn. defeated the 6th Cam. Hdrs. by 3 goals to 2, and qualified thereby for the second round of the First Army Football Cup. In the Army Cross Country Run, the Battn. finished third. Pte.Beattie was third man "home"in the race.	
	28th.		The Commanding Officer completed his inspection of the Battn. In the afternoon the Commanding Officer, Adjutant, Q.M. and T.O. visited the prospective camp at ANTWERP. Through-out the month the Educational Classes were held, and students made considerable progress.	
			Officers. O.R's.	
			7 264.	
			Numbers demobilised during the month.	

C.A.Lockhart. Major,
Commanding,LIVERPOOL SCOTTISH.

Army Form C. 2118.

WAR DIARY
FEBRUARY, 1919, contd.
INTELLIGENCE SUMMARY.

(Erase heading not required.)

Date	Hour	Summary of Events and Information
1919. FEB. 13th.		Coy. & Platoon Training. Application forwarded for Battn. to remain as a Unit in the Army of Occupation, in view of the large number of Other Ranks who were eligible for retention, namely, 1085 O/Ranks.
14th.		Weather much warmer. Coy. & Platoon Training.
15th.		Coys. at disposal of Coy. Commanders. The Battn. boxing team arrived back from the Army Boxing Competition, which had been held at LILLE during the last three days, with many honours, including seven cups. The Officers won the Officers' team prize. 2 Lt. P. BROADHURST won the heavy weight contest. Capt.A.McD.DOUGHTY and 2 Lieut. T.D.J. FINLAYSON were "runners up" in their respective weights. Pte. Stokes won the welter weight contest. In the evening the Officers entertained the Racing Club at dinner, and played a return bridge match with them.
16th.		Voluntary Church Parades. Corp's Cross Country Race was held:- the Battn. team was placed third. The Divl. Football team (4 "Scottish" players included) played the ANTWERP F.C. at ANTWERP, winning by 3 goals to nil.
17th & 18th.		Coys. at disposal of Coy. Commanders for baths and training.
19th.		Coy. training. Semi-final Divl. Rugby Competition. Result:- Battn. 3 points, 1/4th Bn.K.O.R.L. 6 points.
20th and 21st.		Coy. training. Weather continued warm.
22nd.		Battn. drawn against 1/6th Gen. Hdrs. in Army Football Cup Competition. Result, Draw, 2 goals each. Match played at ANTWERP.

Army Form C. 2118.

WAR DIARY

LIVERPOOL SCOTTISH
INTELLIGENCE ~~xx~~ SUMMARY.

(Erase heading not required.)

Instructions regarding War Diaries and Intelligence Summaries are contained in F. S. Regs., Part II. and the Staff Manual respectively. Title pages will be prepared in manuscript.

Place	Date	Hour	Summary of Events and Information	Remarks and references to Appendices
	1919. FEBRUARY.			
	1st.		Battn. still billetted in St.JOB, near BRUSSELS. Coys. at disposal of Coy. Commanders.	
	2nd.		Sunday. Voluntary Church Parades.	
	3rd.& 4th.		Coy. & Platoon Training. Lectures also delivered by Major R.H.D.LOCKHART on the subject of "Armies of Occupation".	
	5th & 6th.		Coys. at disposal of Coy. Commanders for training, baths and delousing. On account of weather recently being so severe Sports could not be held.	
	6th,7th.		2 coys. were engaged in clearing ground from the Rugby Field - Major LOCKHART delivered lectures to the remaining coys.	
	8th.		Coys. at disposal of Coy. Commanders.	
	9th.		Sunday. Voluntary Church parade. Brass Band of 32 O/Ranks arrived from ENGLAND during the evening.	
	10th.		One coy. proceeded to view the famous WATERLOO battle field. In the afternoon the semi-final of the inter-coy. football competition was played. Result:- "X" Coy. 3 goals, "Z" Coy. 2 goals.	
	11th.		Coy. & Platoon training.	
	12th.		B.G.C. addressed Battn. in the School. "Y" Coy. won the Battn. Coy. Football Cup. Final result:- "Y" Coy. 4 goals; "X" Coy. 1 goal. Lt.Col.D.C.D.MUNRO, DSO, MC, DCM proceeded on leave to U.K. and Major R.H.D. LOCKHART assumed command of the Battn.	

contd......

WAR DIARY

10TH LIVERPOOL R

FEBRUARY 1919

WAR DIARY
or
INTELLIGENCE SUMMARY
(Erase heading not required.)

Army Form C. 2118.

Place	Date	Hour	Summary of Events and Information	Remarks and references to Appendices
	1-2-1919.		**REPORT ON BATTN. EDUCATIONAL SCHEME.** (Contd.)	
			In addition to the school curriculum, students who wished to study subjects not taught in the school, have been catered for by courses in Army Workshops. Fitters, turners, blacksmiths, divers, chemists, printers, motor mechanics have attended such courses. The Divisional R.E. School has helped considerably by permitting men to attend special courses there, such as, Building Construction, Electric lighting and power, Mechanics and Machine drawing.	
			The Battn. supplied G.H.Q. School with a special teacher for Agriculture.	
			"Handy men" training has been systematically carried on; tailors, carpenters, pioneers, shoemakers and blacksmiths being attached to respective battn. workshops.	
			Officers are being catered for outside the Battn. area.	
			D.C.Turner	
			Lieut. Colonel, Commanding, LIVERPOOL SCOTTISH.	

WAR DIARY
or
INTELLIGENCE SUMMARY.
(Erase heading not required.)

Army Form C. 2118.

REPORT ON BATTALION EDUCATIONAL SCHEME.

Battn. Educational Officer :- Lt.C.A. WHITE.

Those who wished to take advantage of the Education Scheme came forward voluntarily in October 1918, when the scheme first came into being. At first, the number of students was small (about 90) but as the value of these classes became more evident to the men the numbers increased, until in December 1918 two schools had to be formed, running alternate days, the total number of students being 295.

With a staff comprising trained teachers, the ground covered was sufficient to cater for most needs. As the majority of the students in civil life were clerks the school made a speciality of commercial education, and to this end the following subjects were taught :-

French.   Shorthand.   Book-keeping.   English.   Spanish.
Commercial Course.   Advertising.   Invoicing & Salesmanship.

The results of these courses cannot be gauged other than in the future careers of the students, but if the keenness and interest shown by the men is a criterion, then their business ability will have appreciably increased. 80% of the students merely required refreshment in the various subjects, but the remaining 20% required complete education in elementary school subjects. The latter men necessitated the commencement of tuition in the elementary stages of the following subjects :-

English.   History.   Mathematics.   Geography.

which improvement was noted in tests set weekly, and the men showed themselves keen and thorough in their work.

The encouragement given for the men to visit the billets of their instructors out of school hours met with a satisfactory response.

15 students have entered for the First Class Army Certificate, and are studying these subjects in addition to their business education.

Army Form C. 2118.

WAR DIARY
or
INTELLIGENCE SUMMARY

(Erase heading not required.)

JANUARY 1919. (Contd?)
(3)

Place	Date	Hour	Summary of Events and Information	Remarks and references to Appendices
	Jan. 22nd		Coys at disposal of Coy Commdrs for training. Football match during afternoon between 166 Inf Bde Hqrs and Divnl Arty. Result Bde HQ 1 Arty 0.	
	" 23rd.		Weather very cold. Slight snowfall. Battn Route March. Football during afternoon between against Racing Club. Result LIVERPOOL SCOTTISH 7 to Nil:	
	" 24th.		Coys on M.O's Inspection and Coy Training..	
	" 25th.		Coys on M.O's Inspection and Coy Training. Burn's night celebrated.	
	" 26th.		Weather cold. Some snow. The King of the Belgians took a salute from some representative troops of III Corps. Major R.H.D.Lockhart-6 Subs. and 250 Other Ranks proceeded to Brussels to line the route and assist the M.F.P. A fine spectacle which impressed Brussels very favorably. Voluntary Church parades.	
	" 27th		Weather cold. Heavy snowfall during night. Training and sports impossible owing to snow.	
	" 28th.		Heavy Snow. Coys at disposal of Coy Commdrs. 1/7th K.L.R. versus 166 Bde HQ in final of Divisional League. Result 1/7th K.L.R. 4 Goals Bde HQ 2 Goals.	
	" 29th.		Coys at disposal of Coy Commdrs. Training very difficult on account of weather. Outdoor sports at a standstill.	
	" 30th.		Weather still very cold, no outdoor sports possible.	
	" 31st.		Weather still cold. Sports impossible.	
			REPORT ON EDUCATIONAL SCHEME ATTACHED.	
			Numbers demobilised during January 4 Officers - 150 Other Ranks.	

Lt. Col.
COMMANDING, LIVERPOOL SCOTTISH.

Army Form C. 2118.

WAR DIARY
of
INTELLIGENCE SUMMARY. JANUARY 1919. (Contd)

(Erase heading not required.)

Instructions regarding War Diaries and Intelligence Summaries are contained in F. S. Regs., Part II. and the Staff Manual respectively. Title pages will be prepared in manuscript.

Place	Date	Hour	Summary of Events and Information	Remarks and references to Appendices
	JAN. 11th.		Battalion marched to Hippodrome to view Divisional Cross Country Run. 420 Competitors. In teams - 1 Officer and 29 Other Ranks. 2 Teams supplied by this Battalion. First man home Private Beatty of this Battalion. Private Liddle finished 5th. Our team finished as runners-up to 1/5th K.O.R.L.R.	
	" 12th.		Weather fine. Voluntary Church Parades.	
	" 13th.		Companies at disposal of Company Commanders for baths and training. No sports in the afternoon.	
	" 14th.		Battalion Route Marche through Foret De Toigne. Football during afternoon Inter-Coy Trials. "V" Coy 1. "Y" Coy. Nil.	
	" 15th.		Companies at disposal of Comp and Commanders. Inspection of Lewis Guns by Brigade Inspector. Wet afternoon. No sports.	
	" 16th.		Weather fine and bright. Companies at disposal of Coy Commdrs for training. Inspection of rifles by Lewis Inspector. Rugby Football during afternoon.	
	" 17th.		Companies at disposal of Company Commdrs for Coy and Platoon training. Divisional Boxing Tournament started. Battalion represented by 2 Competitors in each of the following "weights". Feather, Light, Welter and Middle. Also 1 Competitor in the Heavy. Results:	
	" 18th.		Companies at disposal of Coy Commdrs for pay and baths. 2nd Days boxing. Weather fine. Sport during afternoon.	
	" 19th.		Church Parades again voluntary. Rugby during afternoon.	
	" 20th.		All parades cancelled by BGC in view of finals in Divnl Boxing Tournament. Final results. Liverpool Scottish winners of the Cup 35 Pts. 1/5th KORLR 2nd with 32 pts. The Cup was duly christened.	
	" 21st.		Coy at disposal of O.C. Coys. for training. News of death of Prince John recd. Officers' Ball at the Taverne Royal - Brussels. Major Gen Sir Hugh Jeudwine W.S. Regent also & heavy of youth and beauty accompanied by their various Chaperones and cavaliers. Two foursome reels danced which were loudly applauded	

Army Form C. 2118.

WAR DIARY
or
INTELLIGENCE SUMMARY.
(Erase heading not required.)

FEBRUARY. (1)
JANUARY.

Place	Date	Hour	Summary of Events and Information	Remarks and references to Appendices
	Jan 1st.		B.G.C. ordered a holiday. Address to all ranks by the C.O. Association Football match between Officers and Sergeants resulting in win for Officers 2 - 1.	
	" 2nd		Battalion paraded at 10.0am for presentation of medal ribbons by BGC. "other ranks" of this Battalion received ribbons. The Colours were carried "uncased". 1914-15 Star authorised to have same ribbon as 1914 Star.	
	" 3rd		Divisional Inspection by the Divisional Commander General Sir Hugh Jeudwine After inspection the Division marched past the King of the Belgians, The Duke of Teck, Lord Derby and the British Ambassad or were also present. The Regimental Colours were carried uncased. The Battn furnished 5 Officers and 250 Other Ranks for Police Duty at the saluting base. 28 Officers and 850 Others Ranks took part in the March Past. Weather Fine.	
	" 4th.		Companies at disposal of Officers Commanding Companies for Pay &c. Rugby match in the afternoon between Scottish and 422 Field Coy R.E. RESULT Scottish 24 Points R.E.s 6 points.	
	" 5th.		Weather Cold and Showery. Voluntary Church Parades.	
	" 6th.		Companies at disposal of Os /C Coys. for baths, Armorer Sergeant's Inspection. Company and Platoon training, no sports owing to inclement weather.	
	" 7th.		Weather Fine and clear. Companies at disposal of Coy Commanders for training. Football and hockey played during the afternoon. Divisional Swimming Tournament proposed. Major Grey whilst on leave instructed to attend Senior Officers' Course Aldershot.	
	" 8th		Battalion Route march. A platoon and two officers visited Waterloo.	
	" 9th		Companies at disposal of Company Commanders. C.O's parade for all Officers to discuss possible Improvement in Armament and Equipment of an Infantry Battn. Lecture given by the C.O. to "V" Coy on re-enlistment. Hockey match on Roller Sketes against Brussells Team, resulting in win for latter team.	
	" 10th		Weather fine, slight frost. Companies at disposal of Coy Commanders. Rugby Football Match during afternoon. Result Scottish 3 pts 1/5th S.L.R. Nil/	

Army Form C. 2118.

WAR DIARY or INTELLIGENCE SUMMARY

DECEMBER (contd.5)

(Erase heading not required.)

Place	Date	Hour	Summary of Events and Information	Remarks and references to Appendices
	Dec.31st (contd.)		1/5th Bn.K.O.R.L.R. - this Battn. being second, although the first and third men home were of this Battn. The Sergeants' Mess was opened by the Colonel in the evening. The usual Hogmanay ceremonies were duly performed, and the arrival of the New Year was fittingly welcomed, in a manner only known by a Scottish Battn.	
			Numbers who during DECEMBER left Battn. for demobilisation :-	
			1 Officer. 41 Other Ranks.	

M.O. Munro.
Lieut. Col.
Commanding, LIVERPOOL SCOTTISH;

WAR DIARY or INTELLIGENCE SUMMARY.

DECEMBER (contd.4).

Army Form C. 2113.

(Erase heading not required.)

Place	Date	Hour	Summary of Events and Information	Remarks and references to Appendices
	Dec.24th.		The B.G.C. ordered all parades to be cancelled, in order that the men might prepare for Xmas.	
			The following were awarded the Military Medal:-	
			35556.6 CQMS. T.PATTERSON 355661 Pte. J.PIRIE (attachd Bde HQ).	
			358111 L/C. E.C.STANLEY 356918 " A.J.TOWNLEY.	
			53929 Pte. R.E.UNDERWOOD. 359104 " G.LARGE.	
			355220 " G.A.GORTON. 359597 L/C.G.BOND (attachd TMB).	
			The Battn. Officers' Mess was opened with first dinner.	
	Dec.25th.		Xmas Day. Church services held in the morning.	
			After cross-country Run was won by "Y" Coy.	
			Successful Xmas dinners were held at School for "V" and "X" Coys.	
	Dec.26th.		Battn. paraded to witness removal of colours from the Old HQ.Mess to the New Battn. Mess, and then marched past, as this was the first opportunity the Battn. had of viewing same.	
			In dull weather the 55th Divn. Rugby team (captained by Capt. & Adjt. T.G. RODDICK) beat 74th Divn; by 6 points to nil.	
			Lt.E.W.Bird left to be demobilised - the first Officer to get away.	
			Dinners for "Y" and "Z" Coys. held at School.	
	Dec.27th.& 28th.		Coys. at disposal of Coy. Commanders for baths, pay etc.	
	Dec.29th.		Sunday. Usual Church-parades.	
			Team from 55th Divn. played Belgian F.C., and after a stiff struggle beat them by 3 goals to 2.	
			2 Lt. E. HENDERSON awarded the Military Cross.	
	Dec.30th.		Battn. Route March.	
			In the morning, final of Inter-platoon football match played.	
	Dec.31st.		Battn. paraded to witness Brigade Cross Country Run, which was won by the	

Army Form C. 2118.

WAR DIARY
or
INTELLIGENCE SUMMARY.   DECEMBER (contd.).

(Erase heading not required.)

Place	Date	Hour	Summary of Events and Information	Remarks and references to Appendices
	1918.			
	Dec.16th.		Battn. proceeded to SAINTES - a distance of 12 1/2 miles. The march was made tiring by the stone set roads.	
	Dec.17th.		Final destination, St.JOB, reached, after march of 13 miles. Bad roads and weather mitigated aginst good marching.	
			Everyone was pleased with their billets, and were of the opinion that their long stay at St.JOB would prove in every way agreable. The Officers were billetted in mansions, standing in their own grounds, on a hill which overlooked the village below.	
			Col. D.C.D. MUNRO, DSO, MC, DCM, rejoined, and re-assumed command of Battn.	
	Dec.18th.		Battn. engaged in cleaning up.	
	Dec.19th.		Coy. & Platoon Training, Education and Riding Classes.	
			The men, to their great satisfaction, were allowed permanent passes to be absent from their billets, when not on duty, from 1400 hours to 2100 hours daily, for the purpose of proceeding to BRUSSELS.	
	Dec.20.		Advantage was taken of the wet weather, for lectures to be given to the Coys. on "Demobilisation".	
			Rev. Studdert Kennedy lectured in Divl. Theatre on "Demobilisation".	
			Two Officers represented the Battn. at a reception given by the Burgomaster of Brussels.	
	Dec.21st.		Platoon & Coy. Training and Educational Classes.	
			The Divl. Theatres and Cinemas by this time were now all in full swing. 15 O/R's and 2 pipers took part in an Allied tableau at the Opera House, Brussels.	
	Dec.22nd.		Football team, representing 166 Brigade, played against Racing Club, and only just beat the civilians by 5 goals to 4. The game was hotly contested.	
	Dec.23rd.		Platoon & Coy. Training.	
			Enrolment commenced of men eligible to join the "55th Divl. Comrades Assn". The number of students attending Educational Classes now numbered 270.	

Army Form C. 2118.

WAR DIARY
or
INTELLIGENCE SUMMARY.
xxxxxxxxxxxxxxxxxxxxxxxxxx
(Erase heading not required.)

DECEMBER (contd.2)

Instructions regarding War Diaries and Intelligence Summaries are contained in F. S. Regs., Part II. and the Staff Manual respectively. Title pages will be prepared in manuscript.

Place	Date	Hour	Summary of Events and Information	Remarks and references to Appendices
	Dec.9th.		Coy. Training. Battn. played footer match against 2/1st Wessex F.A., and won by 5 goals to 1. Great interest was being shewn in the Platoon Competition (Football), the eliminating games of which were played off every day, when possible.	
	Dec.10th.		Owing to probable move, all ranks were engaged in cleaning up. Later in the day, the move was postponed to a later date. In the afternoon, massed Coy. parades were held, so that ballot papers could be issued and completed. The first men for demobilisation - 10 coalminers - proceeded to England.	
	Dec.11th.		Battn. Route March. Education & Riding Classes. The Battn. Rugby team played against Divl. Hdqrs, and suffered defeat. 5 N.C.O's (including a/RSM.D.A.B.MARPLES,MC,) proceeded to England for tour of duty at home.	
	Dec.12th.		Usual training and classes. Bn.F.C. beat 1/5th K.O.R.L.R. by 2 goals to nil.	
	Dec.13th.		Miserable weather prevailed about this time. Commanding Officer inspected Battn. by coys. In evening, "KinkyRoos" gave a performance at Cinema. Regtl. Colours, with party, arrived.	
	Dec.14th.		Battn. engaged in cleaning up, in preparation for expected move to Brussels area the following day. Owing to abnormal strength of Battn. (1497 All ranks) the Transport at the Battn.'s disposal was totally inadequate to cope with the move, and great difficulty was experienced in getting this matter rectified.	
	Dec.15th.		In fine weather, the Battn. at 1130 hours marched the first stage of the journey to winter quarters, near Brussels. SILLY was reach at 1450 hours, and the Battn. was billetted here for the night. Four German cookers were pressed into Battn. service, and proceeded with the	

Army Form C. 2118.

WAR DIARY
or
INTELLIGENCE SUMMARY
(Erase heading not required.)

Place	Date	Hour	Summary of Events and Information	Remarks and references to Appendices
	1918.			
	Dec.1st.		Battn. billetted at ATH (Belgium). Sunday. Usual church parades.	
	Dec.2nd.		Coy. & Platoon Training. Meeting was held with reference to the proposal to form the "55th Divl. Comrades Association", and representatives attended from this Battn.	
	Dec.3rd.		Battn. Route March. At this time, a Guard of Honour, composed of all decorated men in the Battn., paraded daily for ceremonial training, in readiness of expected visit of H.M. the King, and other notabilities.	
	Dec.4th.		Usual training and Educational Classes. A party set out for ENGLAND to bring the Regimental Colours.	
	Dec.5th.		Coy. & platoon training, Educational and Officers' Riding Classes. R.A.F. Officer delivered an interesting lecture on "Night Bombing". The "Kinky Roos" gave a performance at Divl. Cinema.	
	Dec.6th.		Battn. parade for an hour, the remainder of the morning being devoted to bathing, and cleaning up. Guard of Honour, Educational & Riding Classes paraded as usual. Col.D.C.D.MUNRO, DSO,MC,DCM, proceeded to England for short M.G. Course.	
	Dec.7th.		Battn. paraded at 0800 hours and marched to LIGNE, on main TOURNAI Road. Here the Battn. in conjunction with the remainder of the 55th Division, lined both sides of the road. About 1100 hours, H.M. the KING, dismounting from Royal car, walked through the lines, accompanied by the G.O.C., and followed by retinue, including the Prince of Wales, Prince Albert, General Birdwood and others. There being no ceremony, the Guard of Honour was not called on. The troops gave His Majesty a rousing and loyal reception. At dusk, a draft of 170 Other Ranks arrived.	
	Dec.8th.		Sunday. - Usual Church parades.	

War Diary Vol 48

of

10th Liverpool R

1st to 31st December 1918

1/10th Bn (The King's) Liverpool Regt (Liverpool Scottish)

WAR DIARY
INTELLIGENCE SUMMARY.
(Erase heading not required.)

Army Form C. 2118.

Place	Date 1918	Hour	Summary of Events and Information	Remarks and references to Appendices
9TH	Nov 30th		CASUALTIES OFFICERS OTHER RANKS KILLED IN ACTION — — DIED OF WOUNDS — 1 WOUNDED 1 2 TOTAL 1 3 EFFECTIVE STRENGTH OF BATTALION ON 30/11/18 — OFFICERS 52 O. RANKS 1550 A.C. Allman Lieut. Col. Commanding Liverpool Scottish 30/11/1918.	

Army Form C. 2118.

WAR DIARY
or
INTELLIGENCE SUMMARY.
(Erase heading not required.)

Instructions regarding War Diaries and Intelligence Summaries are contained in F. S. Regs., Part II. and the Staff Manual respectively. Title pages will be prepared in manuscript.

Place	Date	Hour	Summary of Events and Information	Remarks and references to Appendices
ATH	Nov. 1918 30TH		Inspection of Y Company by C.O. 1 Battalion Drill on Esplanade. Parade of Battalion Ranks with Decorations including 1914 Mons Stars, medals. R.S.M. for practice in Guard of Honour. St. Andrew's Day was celebrated. Officers Dinner at 19.30. Hours at Hotel Duquesne. 48 Officers went from unit including Capt. C.K.M. and 2/Lt. Paterson with 166th T.M.B. also Capt. C.B. Davey M.C. and 2/Lt. Cross of Mil. 55th Div. H.Q. Pte Deserved Burns was present and Piper McLean during and after Dinner. Speeches were made after Dinner by Lt. Col. Munro Capt. McGilchrist Rev. Morrison and several other Officers. Pte Satherly was next most entertaining. Pte M.A. and Sergeants also had a Dinner - there were 47 Sergeants present and also 18 Guests from Units in the Division. The morning 1st Battalion Concert Party sang and other Artists gave an excellent programme. Dinner concluded with cheers for the Battalion & King. Speeches written, Band on Billet over by 1st C.O. Howard D.S.O. French & Scottish Airs fully entertaining.	

1/10TH Bn THE KINGS (LIVERPOOL REGT (LIVERPOOL SCOTTISH). Army Form C. 2118.

WAR DIARY
INTELLIGENCE SUMMARY.
(Erase heading not required.)

Place	Date 1918	Hour	Summary of Events and Information	Remarks and references to Appendices
ATH	Nov: 26th		Company Parades.	
	27th		Companies on Working Parties and Private Ventures. Ration lorries TRUNK went to MAPLE COPSE to 276th Artillery Brigade. Return on "Demobilization" by Major Gordon Torrer (G.H.Q) was given in the Theatre ATH at 14:00 hours. On following Officers joined the Battalion Captain D. Howard, Capt W. Phillpots, Capt A.S.T. Houghton, Lieut E.N. Bird, Lieut W.L. Bird.	
	28th		Battalion Parade. Football - Bn. beat 2/1st Lowland Field Ambulance 10 goals - nil. Capt A. McDoughty joined Battalion ex England. Concert Party gave a Performance in Cinema Hall at 17.30 hours. Battalion won the Brigade Boxing Tournament - 43½ points. 15th King's own came 2nd with 41 points.	
	29th		Various Football Matches. Inspection of Companies on Working Parties. Remainder of Battalion on Route March under Major Gray.	

Army Form C. 2118.

1/10th Bn (THE KING'S) LIVERPOOL REGIMENT (LIVERPOOL SCOTTISH)

WAR DIARY

INTELLIGENCE SUMMARY.

(Erase heading not required.)

Instructions regarding War Diaries and Intelligence Summaries are contained in F. S. Regs., Part II. and the Staff Manual respectively. Title pages will be prepared in manuscript.

Place	Date	Hour	Summary of Events and Information	Remarks and references to Appendices
	Nov 1918 20TH		Companies strength under Coy Cmdrs on Railway. Weather very wet. 5th S Rans R. gave a Dance in Theatre Rue de Spectacle at Solesmes. Battalion Rents march. Much sickness in Battalion owing to dampness etc.	
	21st.		Concert Party gave a performance at 1830 hours at 9th Div cinema St Pol.	
	22nd		Battalion at disposal of B.E. Cpm. King of Belgium enters Brussels. Inspection of Officers from Brigade went to Brussels for Parade. Draft of approx. 200 O Ranks arrived from England	
	23rd		Continued at disposal of B.E. Corps.	
	24TH		Church Parades. Memorial Unveiled. (55th Division Memorial) in square at 9th at 1430 hours - a very large gathering. Capt. Davidson given in search of the "incorrigibles" to St Andrews. Night on the 30th Nov.	
	25TH		Another Draft of approx 200 other Ranks arrived from England. Battalion Team played a team of Graham's 17th Divisions (football) and beat them. Bn Team absent (silver Cup) (3) 5 35 p.m. - 1/10th Brigade Reveille. The Cricket Cup from Reserve etc on Battalion Theatre(?)	

(40475) Wt W2555/P360 600,000 12/17 D. D. & L. Sch. 52a. Forms/C2118/15

110th Bn (The King's) Liverpool Regt
WAR DIARY (LIVERPOOL SEPT 1911)
INTELLIGENCE SUMMARY

Army Form C. 2118.

Place	Date	Hour	Summary of Events and Information	Remarks and references to Appendices
	Nov 1918 17th		Battn.B. Football Match in the afternoon versus 422nd Field Coy R.E. won 9 goals to nil. Many prisoners who were liberated witnessed to-day on their way to the Army Base were observed returning & no enthusiasm or notice dull and uninteresting even. British Civilian prisoners to-day on way to Germany through our lines.	
	18th		Companies with Coy Comdrs for Training on Drill Battalion parade cancelled on account of inclement weather. Group party gave performance at 1730 hours - very good show. Football Match in Esperance 165 vs 1/6 S. King - No visible variations 1/12 - 1/12. Photograph taken. Fell officers in Battalion.	
	19th		Companies employed on Railway & Quarry. General Field Hom.B. Work 0900 - 1500 hours. Lectures by Adjutant at 1700 hours on Sword Duties to all Other ranks except Company Commanders. Concert Party gave performance at 1730 hours. Dull day with rain and mist in the afternoon but much warmer. 3 Railway Stations at Brussels reported to have been blown up with 1000 civilian casualties. Two were visited by curious.	

1/10th Bn (THE KING'S LIVERPOOL REGIMENT (LIVERPOOL SCOTTISH))

WAR DIARY

INTELLIGENCE SUMMARY.

(Erase heading not required.)

Army Form C. 2118.

Place	Date	Hour	Summary of Events and Information	Remarks and references to Appendices
	1918 Nov. 15th		Church Parade in Esplanade.	
			Capt. D.D. Farmer VC reported and 6 Officers, with 157 Reinforcements	
			Commenced billeting arrangements for "Y" Coy. who were in Factory.	
			KING ALBERT'S BIRTHDAY was celebrated by a procession through the Town	
			for which all Regts. Bands were requested.	
	16th		Coys. at school & of School & Colours, for cleaning etc. Lt. RATHBONE visited the	
			Theatre in Rue de Spectacle in Grand Place. Previous Brigade held	
			in Rue du Collège. Curfew at 8pm. 2 Sh two at 1700 in A (?) town	
			today. One by bot movement company to tell intervening	
			Brigade Church Parade on Sunday 17th at 10:30 hours. Shots heard in	
	17th		After service at Church, a Brigade Ceremonial parade and march past the G.O.C.	
			to the Church where a Commemoration Service was held. The S.T.?	
			and Brussels Stonewell and Kent were present, also all the	
			civil authorities. The Te Deum was played and the National	
			Anthems of BELGIUM, FRANCE and BRITAIN were played. The Z.O.C.	
			afterwards with a Party inspected the PARIS Church in Belgium	

1/10th Bn (THE KING'S) LIVERPOOL REGIMENT (LIVERPOOL REGIMENT) Army Form C. 2118.

WAR DIARY
or
INTELLIGENCE SUMMARY.
(Erase heading not required.)

Place	Date 1918	Hour	Summary of Events and Information	Remarks and references to Appendices
	Nov 12th		and the weather cleared a little. Throughout the day men were posted at the who had escaped from the Boche were sent in. They continued to come from the "grande route" from BRUSSELS to ATH. The weather was magnificent all day.	
	13th		Companies continued training. 5.O.C. reported the enemy round — but British divisions at 1800 took a drive in the direction Villers... The war zone since — the lives were gone or were frozen. Rain fire was heard all day from a N-South direction. The weather continued good with several degrees of frost at night.	
	14th		B.E.C. met C.O. and Adjutant at 1000 hours and went round billets. Divl. G.O.C. went round at 1200 hours. Still frozen and dry respiration at the Chist once more. The weather continued fine but cold.	
	15th		Battn. less H.Q. & 'B' Coy. lift at 1100 hours and marched in column of route via MAFFLE to ATH. 15th King's Own relieved Battalion in Outpost line. Battalion marched into Billets in ATH. HQ: Mess and	

1/10TH BN. (THE KING'S) LIVERPOOL REGIMENT (LIVERPOOL SCOTTISH)

WAR DIARY
INTELLIGENCE SUMMARY

Army Form C. 2118.

Place	Date	Hour	Summary of Events and Information	Remarks and references to Appendices
	Nov 1918 11th		Battalion then marched through the centre of the town and was marched to ATTRE where we arrived at 15.30 hours. Companies went when billeted in Battalion H.Q. at the Brasserie. The weather was bad all day and cold with a strong breeze crosswind. The Company mess hut for the evening. O.C. in hand friendly during the day. That the hostilities had ceased.	
			O.C. M.S. BENSON and 537. NEEDHAM awarded the MILITARY MEDAL. Companies set to work at once cleaning up etc. Billets consisted of a line of huts in the vicinity occupied by E and W. for the purpose of sheltering all civilians young & retired.	
		16.30	At 14.30 hours there was a celebration of ST MARTIN'S DAY on the Village Square. The remainder of the afternoon and the evening was spent of fiddles and orchestras heard up an enjoy of to various the village band and the police. The effect was exceedingly evident. On the square at 16.30 hours whilst the Church bells rang out as well.	

WAR DIARY
11th Bn (The King's) Liverpool Regiment (Liverpool Regiment)
INTELLIGENCE SUMMARY

Army Form C. 2118.

Place	Date	Hour	Summary of Events and Information	Remarks and references to Appendices
	1918 Nov. 10th		Brigade manages to carry out the 2nd Rehearsal. NOTE. Rehearsing of 276 Bde RFA, 1 Section 55th M.G. Bn. and 1 section 170th Tunnelling Coy RE and 1 section 155th TM.B. attached to us no rehearsed guard.	
	11th		2nd Lieut. T.M. Darrock reported back from sick duty & 30E Gas D.S. Conference of all Officers & Advance Guard at 09.00 hours at Bn H.Q. C.O. went to Conference at 9th Cav Bde H.Q. At 10.35 hours the Commander of the the 55th M.G. Bn came to visit H.Q. and reported that he had seen the officers men that the enemies had been signed. Great excitement. Crowds amongst the troops. The pipes played up and down the village and all the Church bells in the vicinity started ringing. "Y" Company moved off to Advance Guard Rendezvous. Battalion moved off in column of route at 11.45 hours. March on R'HONWELZ to ATH. We crossed the LA DENDRE Riv. by the air bridge which had not been blown up N.W. of ATH. Battalion halted for about 15 minutes by the Church & Battn bivouacked another one night in civilian billets.	

WAR DIARY
or
INTELLIGENCE SUMMARY.

(Erase heading not required.)

Army Form C. 2118.

Instructions regarding War Diaries and Intelligence Summaries are contained in F. S. Regs., Part II, and the Staff Manual respectively. Title pages will be prepared in manuscript.

Place	Date	Hour	Summary of Events and Information	Remarks and references to Appendices
	1918 Nov 10th		wet weather sometime prevented the Troops with Lewis guns to effectually form the screen and machine gunned with the gun crews. The Rifles this bank about 1½ Kilos E of LEUZE in some open fields. HQ. Mess was in a mud house on the main road. Little lunch the Pipe Band returned to LEUZE to play and dance and the Battalion moved on, at Leviers lunch pipers though the Strassen - bivouacs 2 Kilos further on. The first line about 5 Kilos E of LEUZE with Battalion HQ at the station at CHAPPELLE - à - WATTINES. At 16.30 hours orders were received to take up a line 5 Kilos further East. Companies moved independently to new positions - Butt. HQ. eventually established themselves at VILLERS NOTRE DAME. No weather recommendations today - bright sunshine and blue skies with ting of frost in the air. Thermom 7°C. W of LEUZE some thousand refugees were placed pretty today but with the help of civilian salvage the RE's and works folk and mech cat Artillery much thought of both Stockwells force Luncheon	

1/5th Bn. THE KING'S (LIVERPOOL SCOTTISH) Army Form C. 2118.

WAR DIARY
INTELLIGENCE SUMMARY.
(Erase heading not required.)

Place	Date	Hour	Summary of Events and Information	Remarks and references to Appendices
	Nov 1918 9th		Ens	
	10th		Battalion turned out 0500 hours and moved off at 0830 hours. Brigade in 15th Div's advance in column of route. Order and march of King's Own March Forward was at BARRY. The D.S.C. and 2 Coys were of all Officers and Platoon Commanders and Lieut Glen the Stinton and moved nr 279. 9th Cavalry Brigade was 2 Regiments had gone through and First Division on the Brigade's way out Stockwell's force. The Kaiser had abdicated first billeted with Brown Bros. The Americans had taken SEDAN and in that district the Boche was attending guns and stores. He also told us that the objective of the Brigade would be LEUZE in. Continue running SE of LEUZE about 1200 hrs. We continued the march and entered LEUZE about 1200 hrs. Reception was overwhelmed. The streets were everyone with flags and archways of flowers. The people cried the streets cheering and shouting "VIVE LES ANGLAIS" "VIVE LES ECOSSAIS"	

1/10th Bn (The King's) Liverpool Regiment
(Liverpool Scottish)

WAR DIARY
or
INTELLIGENCE SUMMARY

Army Form C. 2118.

Place	Date	Hour	Summary of Events and Information	Remarks and references to Appendices
	1918 Nov. 9th		A return amount of difficulty was found in crossing over the canal and when Battalion arrived. One was on footbridge complete and a pontoon bridge almost completed by 438th Field Coy. R.E. One Company crossed by footbridge, the remaining Companies and transport by the pontoon which was now completed. Battalion then marched via VAULX LEZ TOURNAI to RAMEGNIES where a halt was made to await orders. 1630 hours orders were received to march to billets at SPUTRUT-RAMECROIX. Battalion were billeted in the Distillerie Courturiers in billets along the TOURNAI – LILLE Road. "STOCKWELL'S FORCE" continuing. A Battalion (15th S Lancs) about 1630 hours. Battalion had marched without a halt stopped all the way. In many places the pontoons were built without the erection used to give the appearance of chemical of relief troops. Large numbers of civilians on the road met the Battalion on the way over, the general welcome from the Belgian Flags flying etc. was largely shown almost every window on the road. Posters were issued on behalf of King Albert wishing all British troops flying on Allied Armies Town.	

Army Form C. 2118.

1/10th Bn (KINGS) LIVERPOOL REGT (LIVERPOOL SCOTTISH).

WAR DIARY
or
INTELLIGENCE SUMMARY.
(Erase heading not required.)

Instructions regarding War Diaries and Intelligence Summaries are contained in F.S. Regs., Part II. and the Staff Manual respectively. Title pages will be prepared in manuscript.

Place	Date	Hour	Summary of Events and Information	Remarks and references to Appendices
	1918 Nov 4th		Brigade received Plenipotentiaries. News received that Capt. McSwiney M.C. had died of flu at Oswestry whilst on 6 months leave from duty in France.	
	(Nov. 2nd/1918)		Sergt. McKay awarded CROIX DE GUERRE with Palms.	
ERE.	8th		Received news early in this morning that enemy had commenced to withdraw. Battalion ordered to be prepared to move. Battalion moved about 11.15 hours to ERE marching in column of route. Winter and heavy showers during day but not shelled up towards evening. Battalion ERE for the night, M Coy who were at PONT A RIEU. Slight shelling was between ERE & WILLEMEAU about 1000 hours - evident that the enemy was shelling at tail. Pte Pellots in ERE gave evidence of the hostilities. Destruction wrought by the retreating German. News received that the enemy had been forced up to 1100 hours on the 11th Nov. to accept Terms of Armistice.	
	9th		Battalion paraded at 0830 hours and left ERE at 0900 hours in column of route. First civilians seen on the outskirts of TOURNAI where moving CHERCQ. All bridges over the RIVER ESCAUT were completely demolished.	

(40175) W: W2859/P860 600,000 10/17 D. D. & L. Sch. 52a. Forms/C2118/13

1/10th Bn (THE KING'S LIVERPOOL REGT (LIVERPOOL SCOTTISH)

WAR DIARY
INTELLIGENCE SUMMARY

Army Form C. 2118.

(Erase heading not required.)

Place	Date	Hour	Summary of Events and Information	Remarks and references to Appendices
FROIDMONT	Nov 1918 5TH		Weather fine. B.G.C. inspected the Battalion. Butchers relieved 1/5th S. Lines.	
			No "B" Battalion at FROIDMONT relief carried out without incident. Lt. Jepson.	
			Lectures of a Party from Division which attended the 5th Army Concert Party's	
			performance at the Theatre, LILLE. The concert party was a first-rate	
			during their time out of the line.	
	6TH		Companies at exercise & Coy. Drill for Training. C/Pt. P.O. Gilcrist recalled	
			to Lieut Engineers. Brigade on our left captured 1 officer, 52 O.Ranks	
			3 M.G. and one automatic rifle. Weather fine - heavy rain all day.	
			ITALIAN exhibition arrived at TRIESTE.	
			Concert Party gave a show to Divisional at GYSOING. Padre PIKE proceeded	
			to England on the termination of his engagement.	
	7TH		Companies under Coy Commdrs for training. C.O. proceeded Company Commanders	
			went to reconnoitre in the afternoon. Heavy gas shelling on forward areas	
			all afternoon. Weather dull all day. 2/Lieut Kelly Jones 'V' Company from	
			Dunkirk Reception Camp. Delegates left BERLIN to discuss (6th Nov.)	
			for Conference with Allies on Terms of ARMISTICE. MARSHAL FOCH ambushed	

Army Form C. 2118.

1/10th Battn. (The King's) Liverpool Regiment
WAR DIARY (LIVERPOOL SCOTTISH)
or
INTELLIGENCE SUMMARY.
(Erase heading not required.)

Instructions regarding War Diaries and Intelligence Summaries are contained in F. S. Regs., Part II. and the Staff Manual respectively. Title pages will be prepared in manuscript.

Place	Date 1918	Hour	Summary of Events and Information	Remarks and references to Appendices
ESPLECHIN	NOVEMBER 1st		Companies at disposal of Company Commanders – clearing up Billets etc. The "Kings Roos" Battalion Concert Party gave a show at 1800 hours and their show a first at the time. Weather very poor. Austria capitulates, which were well received by the Troops.	
	2nd		FOOTBALL MATCH: Battalion Team v 166th Fd. A.C. – Lost 2 goals to 5. Concert Party gave another performance at night – complete change of programme including a scene from "OTHELLO" which was very creditable to the performers. The party weather perfect – damp and cold.	
	3rd		Divisional move. The Corps Chess Foot Place – starting point CYSOING. CHURCH PARADES. 2nd Lt LYON proceeded to BETHUNE for surplus stores. Weather held to Lt Col's lunch during the absence. Battalion Concert Party gave their 3rd performance and received a good reception. Lt Col Antrobus M.C. who was Lt Col.	
	4th		Weather exceptionally fine. The Commanding Officer inspected the Battalion at 11:15 a.m. Reports received that 300,000 prisoners & 5,000 guns had been taken by the Italians.	

CONFIDENTIAL

WAR DIARY

OF

10th by LIVERPOOL R

FOR THE PERIOD

1st – 30th NOVEMBER 1918

OCTOBER 1918.   Contd.6.
WAR DIARY.

CASUALTIES.

	Offcrs.	O.R.'s
Killed in Action.	1.	14.
Died of Wounds.		6.
Missing.		41.
Wounded and Missing.		3.
Missing, believed Killed.		1.
Wounded.	4.	58.
	5.	123.

S.T.A. Munro. Lieut. Col.
Commdg. LIVERPOOL SCOTTISH;

Army Form C. 2118.

OCTOBER. 1918.
WAR DIARY
INTELLIGENCE SUMMARY.
Contd. 5.

(Erase heading not required.)

Place	Date	Hour	Summary of Events and Information	Remarks and references to Appendices
	1918. October.			
	23rd.		During the evening, coys. occupied Battle Line of Resistance, and dug in.	
	24th.		Roads and tracks subjected to heavy fire during the night.	
	25th.		Coys. at disposal of Coy. Commanders. The civilains were ordered to evacuate the village. Enemy still holding tenaciously to his line.	
	26th.		Bn. relieved the 1/5th S.LANCS. as Outpost Battn., without incident.	
	27th.		Intermittent shelling of ST.MAUR and ERE.	
	28th.		4 casualties suffered by shell-fire. An enemy aeroplane was brought down in an air-duel, and the pilot (an Officer flight commander) landed in a parachute about 20 yards from one of our posts, and taken prisoner.	
	29th.		Slight shelling of Bn. area. Our artillery very active.	
	30th.		Very heavy shelling during the early hours of the morning, including a heavy gas bombardment. Our artillery carried out continual programmes of harassing fire.	
	31st.		Bn. relieved by 1/5th Bn.K.O.R.L.R. and on relief proceeded to billets in ESPLECHIN. News received, late at night, that TURKEY and AUSTRIA had signed armistice.	

.....contd....

Army Form C. 2118.

OCTOBER 1918.
WAR DIARY
or
INTELLIGENCE SUMMARY. Contd. 4.
(Erase heading not required.)

Place	Date	Hour	Summary of Events and Information	Remarks and references to Appendices
	October 1918.			
	18th.		0900 hrs. found Battn. again on the move, arriving at SECLIN at mid-day. SECLIN, in happier days, must have been a very fine town, but within the last few days had been ruthlessly damaged by the enemy. The civilians had been evacuated some seven days previously, and in their absence all houses had been completely ransacked. Some of the larger chateaux had been gutted by fire. The big church tower had been blown up.	
	19th.		The B.G.C. lectured to all Officers and N.C.O's of the Brigade in the afternoon, but the lecture had to be curtailed somewhat by hurried orders to move. The Battn. spent the night in GD.ENNETIERES. The civilians had not been evacuated from this village, and here the vicious hand of the Boche had been stayed.	
	20th.		At 0830 hrs. the Battn. moved to BOURGHELLES, via CYSOING. En route, the villages were in festal attire, and national flags and bunting, which under the German régime had for so long been consigned to the ignominy of the "lumber room", made gay the streets and houses. This Battn., being the first Scottish soldiers the civilians had seen, came in for particular attention. The unfamiliar skirl of the bag-pipes very quickly brought a throng of sightseers, who stared with curiousity at the swinging kilts.	
	21st.		The Commanding Officer addressed the Battn. at 1000 hrs. The Brigade moved forward to relieve the 165 Brigade in the line; the Battn. relieving the 1/7th Bn. K.L.R. as "B" Battn. at FROIDMONT. On the journey, the Franco-Belgian frontier was crossed at ESPLECHIN.	
	22nd.		Quiet day. Officers and N.C.O's reconnoitred the Brigade front.	

Army Form C. 2118.

OCTOBER 1918
WAR DIARY
or
INTELLIGENCE SUMMARY. Contd. 3.
(Erase heading not required.)

Place	Date	Hour	Summary of Events and Information	Remarks and references to Appendices
	1918. October.			
	9th.		Lt.R.R.AITKEN joined Battn. from ENGLAND. During the night, the Battn. area was subjected to a gas bombardment. 2 casualties.	
	10th.		Our artillery very active. Owing to Divn. side-slipping to the left, the Divn. and Brigade boundaries were accordingly re-adjusted.	
	11th.		Uneventful day.	
	12th.		The Brigade was relieved by 164 Brigade, and proceeded to Divl. Reserve. The Battn. was located in excellent billets in BETHUNE.	
	13th.		Battn. at disposal of Coy. Commanders for pay, indents etc.	
	14th.		Coy. Training.	
	15th.		The "KINKY ROOS" (The Battn. Concert Party) gave their first performance. The show was excellent, and justified their long rehearsals. At 2130 hrs. word was received for the Battn. to hold itself in readiness to move early in the morning. Later definite orders were issued for the move.	
	16th.		Battn. moved at 0630 hrs. by light railway to ILLIES, and thence by march route to MARQUILLIES. The enemy was speedily retiring, closely followed by the forward Brigades.	
	17th.		The action of 5th October was re-constructed under the direction of B.G.C. 2 Lts. R.W.LEWIS, D.H.SANDERS, F.McDONALD, J.F.SHEPHEARDSON, and C.S. PATTERSON, who since their arrival from ENGLAND had been temporarily posted to another unit in the Division, joined the Battn. Soon after mid-day the Battn. moved by march route to ALLENES.	

WAR DIARY Contd. 2.

INTELLIGENCE SUMMARY.

(Erase heading not required.)

Army Form C. 2118.

Place	Date	Hour	Summary of Events and Information	Remarks and references to Appendices
	1918. October. 5th contd.		on far bank of CANAL, and positions held by enemy on near bank. About 1030 hrs. the enemy counter-attacked on the front held by Z Coy. and succeeded in recapturing the positions taken in the early morning. The casualties suffered by "Z" Coy. were exceptionally heavy. Only six N.C.O's and men got back out of two platoons, the remainder being killed, wounded and taken prisoner. "Y" and "X" Coys., who were on the left of the line also suffered heavy casualties, but succeeded in holding their positions. The Battn. was relieved by 1/5th Bn. E. LANCS.Regt at dusk, and became Reserve Battn. distributed as under :- HQrs. and 2 coys. in MARQUILLIES. 1 Coy. " HOCRON. 1 Coy. " PETIT MOISNIL. In two days, in face of considerable opposition, the Battn. advanced the line 1000 yards on the Right, and 2500 yds. on the left. This resulted in driving the enemy outposts back to the line of the CANAL, beyond which progress was impossible, without concerted action by large numbers.	
	6th.		Quiet day. Lt.D.McINTYRE, and 2 Lieuts. A.VERNON and L.CALLANDER joined Battn. from ENGLAND.	
	7th.		Draft of 129 men arrived from B.R.C. to replace casualties suffered in recent action. Enemy artillery engaged in counter-battery work in vicinity of billetting area.	
	8th.		Battn. became "C" Battn. Training was carried out near Coy. billets. Enemy Artillery carry4 shelling of Bn. Area during the night.	

Army Form C. 2118.

WAR DIARY
OCTOBER 1918
INTELLIGENCE SUMMARY.
(Erase heading not required.)

Instructions regarding War Diaries and Intelligence Summaries are contained in F. S. Regs., Part II. and the Staff Manual respectively. Title pages will be prepared in manuscript.

Place	Date	Hour	Summary of Events and Information	Remarks and references to Appendices
	1918 October			
	1st.		Battn. in Support, FESTUBERT Sector, with 2 coys. in O.B.L. and 2 coys. in advance, as close support to Outpost Battn.	
	2nd.		About 1700 hrs. orders were received that the enemy was retiring, and to advance to line occupied by Outpost Battn.	
	3rd.		Early in the morning the Battn. advanced to LA BASSEE - FROMELLES LINE, and later to a line running S.W. - N.E. through PETIT MOISNIL. At dusk, the Battn. relieved the 1/5th Bn.K.O.R.L.R. in Outpost Line. Up to late afternoon, no fighting had ensued. Touch was gained with the enemy about this time on the right, where some shots were exchanged. The Outpost Line extended along a line roughly N.-S. through HOCRON. The relief was accomplished without difficulty. Orders were received from Brigade to continue advance, and cross CANAL, if possible.	
	4th.		During the early morning, coys. pushed forward, and reached a line running N.E. from house in O.2.a. to S.end of BASSE RUE, thence E. to a point in U.22.a.2.2. Heavy fighting went on during the day on the right, where Y coy. had advanced with two platoons to RAILWAY TRIANGLE in U.26.d. They were forced to withdraw from that point by an enemy counter-attack, under cover of heavy machine gun barrage. Some of our own field guns shelled the position held by the platoon on the South side of the Railway, which contributed in a great measure to the enemy success. Machine gun fire was very heavy throughout the whole day, and movement was both difficult and dangerous. About 2020 hours, orders were received from Brigade, giving next day's objective as CANAL BANK, and to cross it if this were found possible. Objectives were allotted to each Coy. and the whole line was advanced about 500 yards, where it was held up owing to heavy machine gun fire from houses	
	5th			

46h

No 46

War Diary
of
10th Liverpool R
for period
1st to 31st October
1918.

Army Form C. 2118.

WAR DIARY
or
INTELLIGENCE SUMMARY.
(Erase heading not required.)

SEPTEMBER (contd.)

Date	Summary of Events and Information	Remarks and references to Appendices
1918.		
Sept. 27th.	Usual training under Coy. Training. Tank demonstration attended by C.O., 2nd i/Cd. Coy. Commanders and C.S.M's.	
Sept. 28th.	Training under Coy. arrangements. Inter-Coy. football matches played, for purpose of selecting Battn. team.	
Sept. 29th.	Sunday, with attendant Church Parades. Lecture given to Officers and N.C.O's by Lt.Col. of Tank Corps on "Co-operation of Tanks with other Arms". The Battn. quietly relieved the 1/5th K.L.R. as "B" Battn. in FESTUBERT Section. Dull weather, culminating in rain about 6 p.m.	
Sept. 30th.	Bn. HQ. shelled about 3 a.m. Left and Right Divisions successfully attacked limited objectives at 6.15 a.m. Official news received at 8 p.m. that Bulgaria had unconditionally surrendered. From midnight, the British Armies in France adopt the continental system of 24 hour clock. During the day, the dispositions of the Coys. had undergone considerable alterations – the general line of Support Battn. being advanced 200 yds. at least. "V" Coy's area at night was subjected to Gas Shell bombardment, and sporadic shelling with 4.2's.	

CASUALTIES.

	Offrs.	O.R's.
Killed.		2
Died of Wounds.		
Wounded.	1	24

J.C. Armour
Lt. Col.

WAR DIARY
or
INTELLIGENCE SUMMARY.
(Erase heading not required.)

Army Form C. 2118.

	Summary of Events and Information	Remarks and references to Appendices
Sept.18th.	Quiet day. Capt. & Adjt. T.G.RODDICK proceeded on leave.	
Sept.19th.	Quiet day.	
Sept.20th.	2 coys. of 1/5th S.LANCS Regt., in conjunction with an attack by Divn. on Left, successfully captured SPOOK TRENCH and PUMPING STATIONS. Divn. on left gained part of LA BASSEE ROAD. In these operations, the S.LANCS. took 46 prisoners, and Divn. on left 76.	
Sept.21st.	To conform with new dispositions, "Y" Coy. side slipped to Right to VIOLAINES VILLAGE.	
Sept.22nd.	Rainy weather. Enemy successfully counter-attacked Gloucester Regt.(Divn. on Left) and captured 2 platoons. "X" Coy., to conform with the situation thus formed withdrew 2 platoons, to drain in front of LA TCULOTTE FARM. 2 Lt. F.HUGHES wounded. "V" Coy. L.G. Post (L/C. E.C.STANLEY in charge) routed two hostile parties, which attempted to approach post, by L.G. fire. Sgt.QUINN ("V" Coy.) ran into enemy patrol, and shot the officer, making good his escape. At 9 p.m. S.O.S. went up on Left of Battn., to which Artillery responded. No enemy action developed.	
Sept. 23rd.	Aerial activity. 2 Lt. H.RIDEHALGH killed by enemy sniper. Battn. on relief by 1/6th K.L.R. proceeded by train to billets in BETHUNE.	
Sept.24th - 25th.	Days devoted to cleaning up, pay, indents etc. Excellent billets.	
Sept.26th.	Usual training. 1/6th Bn.K.L.R. - in co-operation with Divn. on Left - attacked and captured PIONEER DUMP, DISTILLERY and portions of LA BASSEE ROAD. Enemy immediately counter-attacked, and were repulsed.	

Army Form C. 2118.

WAR DIARY
or
INTELLIGENCE SUMMARY.
(Erase heading not required.)

	Summary of Events and Information	Remarks and references to Appendices

1918.

Sept. 10th. Improved weather.
Chile ST. ROCHE subjected to Gas Shell bombardment.
"Y" Coy. had 1 N.C.O. and 6 men badly burnt through Bosche 'booby' trap.
Lt.G.A.WHITE and 2 Lts. F.HUGHES and J.S.SPENCE joined Battn.

Sept. 11th. Inclement weather. Front line heavily shelled at dawn.
Lt.Col.D.C.D.MUNRO, DSO, MC, DCM., returned from leave.

Sept. 12th. Intermittent shelling of "Z" House, during the afternoon.
Lt. G.GREAVES was accidentally injured whilst on patrol, and was evacuated to hospital.

Sept. 13th. Battn. Sniper 'bagged' a Bosche in LA BASSEE ALLEY.
At dusk the Battn. was withdrawn into Support.
Dispositions of the Brigade changed, and the Brigade front is now held by
"A" Battn. ------ OUTPOST LINE.
"B" " ------ SUPPORT.
"C" " ------ RESERVE.

Sept. 14th. Brigade on Right attacked CANTELEUX TRENCH with partial success.

Sept. 15th. Eventless day. Lt.Col.D.C.D.MUNRO, DSO, MC, DCM., took over command of 166 Brigade during the temporary absence of the Brigadier.

Sept. 16th. Enemy artillery active.
Divn. on left (16th) took LA TOULOTTE FARM.

Sept. 17th. Battn. Hdqrs. moved forward to BUCK POST.
At 5.25 a.m. the Right Brigade, in co-operation with attack by Divn. on Right, attacked limited objectives. Right Brigade cleared CANTELEUX TRENCH of enemy.
American M.O. (Lt.HINTON) was temporarily attached to Battn. during absence of Cpt.RICE, on leave.

Army Form C. 2118.

SEPTEMBER 1918.
WAR DIARY
INTELLIGENCE SUMMARY.
(Erase heading not required.)

	Summary of Events and Information	Remarks and references to Appendices
1918.		
Sept. 1st.	Battn. in front line, Right sub-sector, Festubert Section. Quiet day.	
Sept. 2nd.	During the early hours, there were indications of enemy withdrawal. About 9 a.m. the Battn. Scouts went out, and failed to obtain contact with the enemy. A platoon of "Z" Coy. was pushed forward and occupied GEORGE STREET and LOOP ROAD - their right flank being in touch with 1/6th Bn.K.L.R. whose patrols had penetrated into Chile ST. ROCHE. Our patrols continued to push East and North. without getting into contact with enemy. At 3 p.m. a platoon of "Y" Coy. occupied the O.B.L. as far as BARNTON ROAD. At dusk, the Battn. was relieved by 1/7th K.L.R., and proceeded by bus to VAUDRICOURT CAMP No.2.	
Sept. 3rd.	Battn. engaged in cleaning up, pay, bathing etc. 165 Brigade occupied DOVER TRENCH.	
Sept. 4th.	Usual training carried out. Lt.Col. LEWIS, F.A.F., lectured to Officers and Men on "Co-operation of Infantry with Aircraft".	
Sept. 5th.	Brigade Tactical Scheme.	
Sept. 6th.	Holiday. Platoon Football matches played off.	
Sept. 7th.	Battn. at disposal of O's.C.Coys.	
Sept. 8th.	Battn. moved up to relieve the 1/7th K.L.R. Heavy showers of rain.	
Sept. 9th.	Eventless day. A.R.O. (announced the award of the Military Cross to Lt. P.St.J.B.RATHBONE (away on leave).	

War Diary
of
10th Liverpool R
for 1 Rencor
1st to 30th September
1918.

Army Form C. 2118.

WAR DIARY
INTELLIGENCE SUMMARY

(Erase heading not required.)

	Summary of Events and Information	Remarks and references to Appendices

1918. 31st Aug.	Four daylight patrols out. Two enemy sentries were shot, and a new post established 80 yards further North up O.B.L., which latter by 10 p.m. was consolidated and wired. Enemy during night made no attempt to neutralise this encroachment.
	
	A conspicuous feature of the last two months has been the activity of the Bn. daylight patrols (Snipers and Scouts) under the able leadership of Lt. P. StJ. B. RATHBONE.
	Highly appreciative comments on the invaluable information obtained, and the excellent work accomplished have been several times been received from Corps, Divisional and Brigade Commanders.
	As showing the dash and resource displayed in the execution of these exploits, two Military Medals were gained - one by 356372 Pte. N. TANNER (Scout) and the other by 356120 Pte R. BURTON (Sniper).
	
	CASUALTIES.
	
	                    Offcrs. O.R's.
	Killed. - 8
	Died of Wounds. - 2
	Wounded. 1 5
	     Total. 1 15
	
	James Gray, Major,
	Commanding, LIVERPOOL SCOTTISH.	

Army Form C. 2118.

10th (Scottish) Bn. K.L.R.

WAR DIARY

INTELLIGENCE SUMMARY

(Erase heading not required.)

	Summary of Events and Information	Remarks and references to Appendices
1918.		
24th Aug.	Misty morning favoured operation against craters and part of O.B.L., which has been in enemy hands since April. This Bn. was not directly engaged. Zero hour:- 7.20 a.m. At 7.50 a.m. news was received that objectives had been gained with little resistance. The operation was entirely successful – 46 prisoners captured and enemy casualties reckoned at 150, including 4 officers. Our casualties were approx. 100. At 8.10 a.m. and 9.35 a.m. enemy timidly counter-attacked and easily repulsed. Heavy shelling continued throughout day. At night 2 Platoons of the Bn. were sent up to O.B.L. to assist in consolidating and wiring new positions.	
25th Aug.	Enemy quiet. Bn. quietly relieved 1/5th King's Own R.L.R. in Le PLANTIN sector – "Z" Coy; were distributed in part of O.B.L., captured day previous. Some shelling of Bn. Area during night.	
26th - 27th Aug.	Dispositions around CHESHIRE ROAD were readjusted somewhat. Very quiet day.	
28th Aug.	Daylight patrol located enemy post and, after having shot the sentry, bombed the post. Enemy active with harassing fire.	
29th Aug.	Capt. H.T. WHITSON was seriously wounded in early morning. Quiet day. A Proposal for the occupation of O.B.L. to BARNTON TRENCH was well in hand and the Bn. Operation Order had been dictated; Brigade cancelled same and later only postponed it.	
30th Aug.	Quiet day. During night enemy bombed extreme right post of right Front Coy and the assailants were dispersed by rifle fire.	

1/10th (SCOTTISH) Bn. K.L.R.

WAR DIARY
or
INTELLIGENCE SUMMARY.
(Erase heading not required.)

Army Form C. 2118.

	Summary of Events and Information	Remarks and references to Appendices
1918.		
13th Aug.	Our Artillery engaged all day in cutting enemy wire on Divisional Front. Heat excessive. Leave allotment increased to 6 per day.	
14th Aug.	Bn. daylight patrol active in vicinity of BARNTON ROAD. Right Brigade Front heavily bombarded for 15 minutes, about 7 p.m.	
15th Aug.	Quiet day. Our Artillery continued their wire-cutting programme. Bn. relieved by 1/5th K.L.R. and moved to "Bustle" positions.	
16th Aug.	At 3 a.m., the enemy opened out a heavy bombardment on the whole Divisional Front; Trench Mortars co-operating. The shelling died down about 5 a.m. without any sequel, and Bn. stood down and proceeded to billets at No. 1 Camp, VAUDRICOURT. Reveille 12 noon - remainder of day devoted to cleaning up, pay etc., Officers and N.C.Os. attended lecture on co-operation of R.A.F. with other arms.	
17th Aug.	Bn. at disposal of Company Commanders.	
18th Aug.	Sunday. Usual Church Parades.	
19th Aug.	Officers and N.C.Os. attended B.G.C's demonstration. Brigade Boxing Competition held. Bn. won middle weight contest (L/c G.W. PHILLIPS).	
20th Aug.	Commanding Officer's inspected Bn. at 11 a.m. Bn. moved up to relieve 1/6th Bn. K.L.R. in Support.	
21st-23rd Aug.	Hot weather. Uneventful days.	

Army Form C. 2118.

1/10th (SCOTTISH) Battn. K.L.R.

WAR DIARY

INTELLIGENCE SUMMARY.

(Erase heading not required.)

	Summary of Events and Information	Remarks and references to Appendices
1918.		
1st Aug.	Bn. in DROUVIN CAMP; usual training programme carried out. In the evening Bn. Boxing Tournament was held.	
2nd Aug.	Proposed Brigade Tactical Scheme was abandoned in consequence of heavy rain.	
3rd Aug.	Bn. relieved, without incident, the 1/5th Bn. K.L.R. in CAILLOUX Sector.	
4th Aug.	Enemy quiet until 10 p.m., when he placed a heavy barrage on S.O.S. lines for an hour. Two casualties were suffered.	
5th Aug.	Quiet day. ADDISON ROAD received slight attention at dusk.	
6th Aug.	Slight intermittent shelling.	
7th Aug.	Daylight Patrol, under Lieut RATHBONE, located enemy post N. of CAILLOUX. Close approach was rendered impossible through wire, but patrol had satisfaction of shooting sentry. Bn. on relief by 1/5th King's Own R.L.R. proceeded into Support. Harassing fire during the relief was responsible for a few casualties.	
8th Aug.	Quiet day. Arrival at Divisional Reception Camp, reported of personnel of American Training Staff and 274 O/Rs (Details of 2nd Bn.) who have been at Base since amalgamation.	
9th Aug.	Major J. GRAY, M.C., 1/4th Royal Scots arrived and assumed duties of Second in Command.	
10th Aug.	Considerable aerial activity. LONE FARM and Bn. H.Q. shelled.	
11th Aug.	Bn. moved up to Right sub-sector to relieve 1/5th S. Lancs. Regt.	
12th Aug.	Front Line received attention between 10 and 11 a.m.	

Vol 44

44h

War Diary
of
10th Rhode R
for period
1st to 31st August
1918.

Army Form C. 2118.

WAR DIARY
or
INTELLIGENCE SUMMARY.
(Erase heading not required.)

Instructions regarding War Diaries and Intelligence Summaries are contained in F. S. Regs., Part II. and the Staff Manual respectively. Title pages will be prepared in manuscript.

Place	Date	Hour	Summary of Events and Information	Remarks and references to Appendices
	26th July.		Early morning Trench Mortar activity on Battn. Area. Daylight patrol under 2/Lt RATHBONE succeeded in penetrating the enemy day post line. An attempt to "rush" a post was frustrated. One German was shot at close range. Heavy enemy M.G. fire was brought to bear on the patrol. The patrol succeeded in returning to our line - one man slightly wounded.	
	27th July.		Heavy rain. The enemy wire and posts located in yesterday's daylight patrol were heavily shelled with Hows.	
	28th July.		Battn was relieved, without incident, by 1/7th Bn. K.L.R. and proceeded into "Bustle" position.	
	29th July.		Arrived in DROUVIN Camp 5.30 a.m. Reveille 12.30 p.m. Remainder of day spent in cleaning up, etc.	
	30th/31st July.		Usual training carried on, special attention being paid to wiring demonstration in view of forthcoming competition, also to a detachment which has been chosen to represent Battn. on Sunday, August 4th, at Corps Commemoration Service.	

CASUALTIES.

	Offcrs.	O.R's.
Killed.	-	-
Missing.	1.	-
Wounded.	1.	14.
	2.	14.

A. Munro
Lt. Col.,
Commanding, 1/10th (Scottish) Bn. K.L.R.

Army Form C. 2118.

WAR DIARY
or
INTELLIGENCE SUMMARY.

Instructions regarding War Diaries and Intelligence Summaries are contained in F. S. Regs., Part II. and the Staff Manual respectively. Title pages will be prepared in manuscript.

Place	Date	Hour	Summary of Events and Information	Remarks and references to Appendices
	16th/17th July.		(Cont'd) Advice received that Division on Left reported abnormal enemy movement, and all precautions were taken, but nothing transpired.	
	18th July.		Quiet day. Work was principally concentrated on the laying of duckboards on the submerged tracks.	
	19th July.		Some aquatic sports were held in the morning for the benefit of H.Q. personnel.	
	20th July.		Enemy continued quiet. The Battn. moved up to relieve the 1/5th South Lancs. in the FESTUBERT Sector; which relief was completed without incident. "Y" and "Y" Companies were front line Companies. One Company of 36th Bn. Northumberland Fusiliers (B1 men) were was attached to Battn for instructions - a platoon being attached to each Company.	
	21st July.		Very little hostile activity. The Company of Northumberland Fusiliers attached to Battn withdrawn during the night.	
	22nd July 23rd July		Quiet days	
	24th July.		At 3 a.m. the enemy raided ESSARS sector, and the whole of the Battn. area expected experienced a heavy shoot of Trench Mortars, 4.8's and 5.9's, which lasted until 4.50 a.m. No casualties were suffered and little damage was done to the trenches. A daylight patrol penetrated 350 yards into No Man's Land and successfully located enemy day post.	
	25th July.		Slight shelling of Battn. Area. Weather very unsettled.	

Army Form C. 2118.

WAR DIARY
or
~~INTELLIGENCE SUMMARY~~

Instructions regarding War Diaries and Intelligence Summaries are contained in F.S. Regs., Part II. and the Staff Manual respectively. Title pages will be prepared in manuscript.

Place	Date	Hour	Summary of Events and Information	Remarks and references to Appendices
	12th July.		A very successful Brigade Horse Show and Fete was held in VAUDRICOURT Chateau Grounds. The 1/5th King's Own Royal Lancaster Regiment carried off the Cup for aggregate points – the Battn. tieing with Brigade H.Q. for second place. The Scottish were awarded first prize for best ordinary horse, Company Commanders' horse and water-cart, and took second prize with cooker. The Major General distributed the prizes at the conclusion.	
	13th July.		About 10.30 a.m., the camp was startled by the unexpected arrival of a salvo of 4.2's from an enemy H.V. gun. The shells fell just behind the Camp near the road. This shelling continued at intervals until 9 p.m. The Battn. was fortunate in sustaining only 4 casualties – including Major Cunningham who was wounded in forearm. The Corps Artillery carried out counter-shoot on enemy battery. The Battn. slept the night in trenches in vicinity of Camp, but no further shelling was experienced.	
	14th July.		Sunday. The H.V. gun was busy again in vicinity of VERQUIN FOSSE but none disturbed the serenity of the Camp. The Brigade assembled for Divine Service after which the G.O.C. distributed decorations gained by members of the Brigade during the operations commencing April 9th.	
	15th July.		B.G.C. addressed all Officers & N.C.O's, and subsequently the Commanding Officer addressed the Battalion. Night 15th/16th the Battn. quietly relieved the 1/5th Bn. K.L.R. in support in LePLANTIN – HUBERT Sector. At midnight several shells (106 fuze) fell in vicinity of Battn H.Q.	
	16th/17th July.		In consequence of heavy rains during the last few days the tracks and roads in this marshy and flat region were in many cases nearly impassable. Quiet day. Between 11 p.m. and 2 a.m. Battn H.Q. was again subjected to shelling by 4.2's (106 fuze). The CANAL BANK also received attention.	

WAR DIARY
INTELLIGENCE SUMMARY

Army Form C. 2118.

Instructions regarding War Diaries and Intelligence Summaries are contained in F.S. Regs., Part II. and the Staff Manual respectively. Title pages will be prepared in manuscript.

Place	Date	Hour	Summary of Events and Information	Remarks and references to Appendices
	1918.			
	1st July.		Battn. in trenches in LE PLANTIN Sector. Slight intermittent shelling of Battn. area. A patrol which went out at night encountered strong enemy patrol and after an exchange of rifle shot withdrew. On return to trenches, 2/Lt. A.T.C. MYLES, patrol leader found to be 'missing.' (K)	
	2nd & 3rd July.		Slight shelling of Battn. Area. Enemy low flying aeroplanes active. Weather overcast.	
	4th July.		Tactical Exercise on Brigade Defence Scheme. Corps and Divisional Commanders present. Inter-Company relief.	
	5th July.		Quiet day. Poor visibility. Our artillery opened up very heavy, harassing fire about 10 p.m. which continued up to midnight.	
	6th July.		Very little shelling.	
	7th July.		At night artillery heavily bombarded suspected enemy post in ruined houses. Patrol later searched bombarded area but found no trace of enemy casualties. Bosche N.C.O's pack and greatcoat brought back.	
	8th July.		Quiet Day.	
	9th July.		Enemy heavily shelled selected targets in Battn. Area in early morning - for which our artillery effectively retaliated. Enemy shelling ceased about 5 a.m. Battn. (less 2 half-coys.) relieved by 7th Bn. K.I.R. and proceeded to "Bustle" positions. Two half-Companies were left in line as garrison for Bridgeheads.	
	10th July.		Reveille 11.30 a.m. Remainder of day spent in cleaning-up, pay, etc.	
	11th July.		Training carried out by Companies not engaged on working parties.	

Army Form C. 2118.

WAR DIARY
or
INTELLIGENCE SUMMARY.
(Erase heading not required.)

JUNE 1918. (continued).

Place	Date	Hour	Summary of Events and Information	Remarks and references to Appendices
	June 29th.		Weather warm, but poor visibility. HQ. shelled with five rounds of 106 fuze 'whizz-bangs'. Enemy very quiet.	
	June 30th.		Sunny weather. Front very quiet. GORRE received slight artillery attention. The Battn. relieved the 1/5th Bn.K.O.R.L. Regt.in LE PLANTIN Sub-sector without incident, about midnight.	

CASUALTIES.

	Offcrs.	O/R's.
Killed in Action.	1.	9.
Died of Wounds.	1.	2.
Wounded.	2.	27.
	4.	38.

R.Cunningham. Major,
Commanding, 10th (SCOTTISH) Battn. K.L.R.

Army Form C. 2118.

WAR DIARY
or
INTELLIGENCE SUMMARY.

JUNE 1918.

(Erase heading not required.)

Instructions regarding War Diaries and Intelligence Summaries are contained in F. S. Regs., Part II. and the Staff Manual respectively. Title pages will be prepared in manuscript.

Place	Date	Hour	Summary of Events and Information	Remarks and references to Appendices
	June 20th.		At 11.15 night 19/20th Brigade on right raided enemy post, and brought back a prisoner. From 2.45 - 3.45 a.m. enemy opened a general bombardment on battn. area, to which our artillery vigorously retaliated, until enemy artillery quietened down about 4 a.m. CAILLOUX again received marked attention.	
	June 21st.		Battn. relieved by 1/6th Bn.K.L.R. and proceeded for night to positions in rear of "BUSTLE" area. The Brigadier proceeded to ENGLAND on leave, and the command of the Brigade devolved on Lt.Col.D.C.D.MUNRO, D.S.O., M.C., D.C.M. Major R.CUNNINGHAM, M.C. assumed command of the Battn.	
	June 22nd.		At 5 a.m. the Battn. stood down, and proceeded to No. 2 Camp, VAUDRICOURT. Officers reconnoitred "BUSTLE" areas, while the men were engaged on cleaning up, pay etc. During the last two days several men on Bn. Hdqrs. complained of slight headaches, and high temperatures, but the origin of the 'fever' was unknown.	
	June 23rd - 26th.		Battn. engaged in training. One coy. each day was employed on working parties. This period was chiefly remarkable for an epidemic of influenza which broke out. Over 200 men had to be evacuated to hospital. The symptoms were headaches and high temperatures. C.R.O. alluded to same as "Three day Fever". The Battn. being so weakened in numbers did not leave any battle details behind on proceeding to line to relieve the 1/6th Bn. K.L.R. in Support, night 26th/27th June.	
	June 27th.		Slight aerial activity. Usual working parties out at night.	
	June 28th.		Heavy bombardment opened in the early hours away on Battn's left, increasing to 'drum-fire' between 5 a.m. and 6.30 a.m. Later this was confirmed as a prelude to a successful minor operation undertaken by British Troops in the vicinity of FORET de NIEPPE. An advance of 1,500 yds. was made on a 3500 yds front. 400 prisoners and 22 machine guns were captured. Remainder of the day passed without incident.	

Army Form C. 2118.

WAR DIARY
or
INTELLIGENCE SUMMARY.

(Erase heading not required.)

JUNE 1918 (contd).

Place	Date	Hour	Summary of Events and Information	Remarks and references to Appendices
	June 12th. to 13th.		Fresh enemy post located by 2 Lt. HUGHES and patrol. One of our aeroplanes was driven down near CAILLOUX. The pilot and observer escaped unhurt into our lines At night the Battn. was relieved by 1/5th S.Lancs. Regt. and proceeded into Support. Lt. HUGHES took out fighting patrol with intention to try if possible to obtain an identification from the new post discovered previous night. His attempt was unsuccessful - owing to enemy being on 'qui vive'	
	June 14th.		Weather cold but fine. Raid was carried out by 165 Brigade - 2 prisoners captured. Announced that Col.D.C.D.MUNRO, M.C., DSM, had been awarded the D.S.O. 2Lt.L.A.DAVEY and Capt.W.E.RUSHBY (R.A.M.C. - M.O. to Bn. during operations on and about April 9th) were awarded each a bar to M.C. 2 Lt. T.W.PILKINGTON received M.C. Sgt.A.BAYBUT received bar to D.C.M., and Sgt. D.McRae D.C.M.	
	June 15th.		Bn. engaged on working parties at night.	
	June 16th.		Weather much warmer, but showery. The Bn. relieved without incident 1/5 K.O.R.L. Regt. in FESTUBERT Sector.	
	June 17th.		Bursts of 4.2 on Bn. Hdqrs. at DUKES POST. Intermittent shelling of whole Battn. sector during the day. Hostile artillery quietened towards dusk. Our A.A.L.G's during the day had been busy engaging low flying enemy aircraft.	
	June 18th.		Persistent shelling of CAILLOUX. Platoon Hdqrs. totally destroyed. 2 Lt. W.R.KELLIE, batman, Signaller and two others killed outright. FESTUBERT also received considerable attention from 5.9s, delayed action. Our artillery retaliated vigorously for enemy liveliness.	
	June 19th.		At 12.35 a.m. the Divn. on our left carried out successful enterprise, and captured 3 prisoners. At 1.10 a.m. 1/5 S.Lancs. Regt. unsuccessfully raided enemy trenches opposite LE PLANTIN, no identifications being obtained. The Battn. area during these operations naturally received considerable enemy attention. The remainder of the day enemy artillery was negligible.	

Army Form C. 2118.

10th Kings Liverpool Regt.
(Liverpool Scottish)

WAR DIARY
or
INTELLIGENCE SUMMARY.
(Erase heading not required.)

JUNE 1918

Instructions regarding War Diaries and Intelligence Summaries are contained in F.S. Regs., Part II. and the Staff Manual respectively. Title pages will be prepared in manuscript.

Place	Date	Hour	Summary of Events and Information	Remarks and references to Appendices
	June 1st.		The early hours of the morning were marked by hostile artillery activity - gas shells being freely used. Capt. A.P.DICKINSON, M.C. was wounded whilst inspecting his front line posts; and died of wounds a few hours later. Four other casualties were sustained. The Battn. (less 2 half-coys, left as garrisons for Bridge-heads) was relieved by the 1/6th Bn.K.L.R. during the evening, and proceeded to "BUSTLE" positions.	
	June 2nd.		After 'stand-down' at 5 a.m. the Battn. (less 2 half-coys) moved to No.2 Camp, VAUDRICOURT. Day devoted to cleaning up etc. Capt. DICKINSON was buried at HOUCHIN.	
	June 3rd.-5th.		Mornings devoted to training: the afternoons to recreation.	
	June 6th.		Battn. marched to DROUVIN, and practised an Advance Guard, and Open Order Attack. Prisoners obtained in the line about this period stated an enemy attack on this front was imminent. Battn. was under half-an-hour's notice.	
	June 7th.		Lectures on Bayonet Fighting and Gas, under Brigade arrangements. Brigade Fête held in Chateau grounds.	
	June 8th.		Col.de la Poer, H.A. delivered interesting lecture on Counter-Battery work to all Officers, and the Brigadier followed with an address.. The Battn. Concert Party gave an excellent performance to a crowded audience in Y.M.C.A. Hut. Battn. relieved 1/6 K.L.R. in LE PLANTIN sector. Relief completed without enemy interference.	
	June 9th.		From 3 a.m. to 4:30 a.m. GIVENCHY area was subjected to a heavy gas shell bombardment (Yellow and Blue Cross). This Battn. only sustained few casualties - but the units in 165 Brigade suffered severely. 50 rounds 4.2 fell in vicinity of Bn. HQ. about noon. Our heavies active.	
	June 10th.		Enemy artillery fairly quiet. Bn. Hdqrs. moved back to BATTERSEA BRIDGE gunpits.	
	June 11th.		Enemy patrol activity "nil". Our 'dawn' patrol brought in three Portuguese prisoners of war, who were coming into our lines. Day generally quiet.	

War Diary
of
10th Liverpool R
for period
1st to 30th
June 1918

Army Form C. 2118.

WAR DIARY
or
INTELLIGENCE SUMMARY.
(Erase heading not required.)

Place	Date	Hour	Summary of Events and Information	Remarks and references to Appendices
Inkerfield	28/5/18		Battn relieved 1/5 Kings Own R.L. Regt in the Le PLANTIN South section — relief being completed without incident.	
	29/5/18		Enemy artillery fairly quiet. Enemy aeroplane dropped 6 explosive bombs. Hostile Balloon opposite Battn front brought down in flames.	
	30/5/18		About 2.30 am enemy put down a heavy barrage on front CAILLOUX — ROUTE A KEEP, and raided the Battn on left. He was repulsed. Remainder of day quiet.	
	31/5/18		Renewed hostile artillery activity — 8" being reported at ESTAMINET CORNER	

Total casualties for the month:—

	Officers	Other Ranks
Killed and Died of wounds	Nil	7
Wounded	Nil	34
		41

R.C.D. Munro
Lt Col Comdg
1/10 (Scottish) Bn K.L.R.

Army Form C. 2118.

WAR DIARY
or
INTELLIGENCE SUMMARY.
(Erase heading not required.)

Place	Date	Hour	Summary of Events and Information	Remarks and references to Appendices
In the field	31/5/18		13/5/18 (cont) Capt R.D CUNNINGHAM M.C. who has been commanding the Battn was evacuated to Hospital and Lt.Col. D.C.S MUNRO M.C. D.S.M. was sent for from Battle details to take over command. 14/5/18 Bn was relieved by 1/5 K.R.R. and from to proceed to camp at VAUDRICOURT, occupied "BUSTLE" positions in LE PREOL and remaining 15/5/18 "Stand down" received at 5.45 a.m. when Battn proceeded to clean up Battn was ordered at ½ hours notice. 16/5/18 Day occupied in cleaning up, bath and re-organisation. 17/5/18 Training-particularly work under the supervision Brigade M.G. Corpsl in musketry. 18/5/18 + 19/5/18 Training so far as in the evening by Battn. Coved Party. 20/5/18 Battn. returns 17 K.L.R. in the FESTUBERT left sub-sector - relief being satisfactorily completed by 1.30am. 21/5/18 FESTUBERT CENTRAL receives attention in enemy "minnies" - four direct hits being obtained. Enemy hostility. Shells GORRE with gas shells. 22/5/18 Low flying enemy aeroplane fires over the lines in the early morning, firing into our trenches. Enemy activity very active during day. 23/5/18 VILLAGE LINE shelled intermittently. 24/5/18 Battn. relieved by 4/5 SOUTH LANCS RGT & moves into support positions 25/5/18 TUNING FORK, & ROAD and ESTAMINET corner heavy shells during the day. 26/5/18 LONE FARM shelled. Rest of front quiet. 27/5/18 Enemy channel very active - engaged by our Lewis and machine guns; BATTERSEA BRIDGE was shelled and a direct hit obtained on the bridge.	

May 1918

WAR DIARY
or
INTELLIGENCE SUMMARY.
(Erase heading not required.)

Army Form C. 2118.

Place	Date	Hour	Summary of Events and Information	Remarks and references to Appendices
Unkefields	31/5/18		Battn in camp at VAUDRICOURT on 1st May. The remainder of the HLD (COSH?) B" K.L.R. were inspected by the Brig. Genl. Comndg in the morning and in the afternoon marched off to the Div. Rampoument camp at BLOQUVE	BD/1
	2/5/18		Battn "stood to" between 3.30am and 7.0 am at nine the B.G.C. addresses the officers of the Brigade on work in trenches to. The same evening, Battn relieves 17 K.L.R. in the FESTUBERT left sub-section - relief being completed	
				4-5-6/18
	6/5/18		Enemy quiet. A prisoner, belonging to the 10th R.R was captured by Z Coy. He had, apparently lost his way and walked into our lines.	
	7/5/18		The Battn was relieved by 1/5 SOUTH LANCS R. and moves into support positions in the LE PRÉOL vicinity 2nd Lieut. T W THOMSON reports for duty.	8/5/18 Patrol...(?) in
			progress from our trenches. A probable enemy attack - which was to take place on the 9th or 10th inst - devors (?) and to information. Our artillery very active here, shelling given by a prisoner. Enemy amount very both enemy's front and back areas.	
	10/5/18		Quiet throughout the day. Quiet night. No Right sub section relieves 1/5 KINGS OWN R. and R---	
	11/5/18		Enemy amount again active. Our own artillery fire continuous throughout the night. Otherwise quiet.	
	12/5/18		Very quiet, except for a little artillery fire on GoR sides.	
	13/5/18		A few casualties sustained in a patrol of enemy (?) on our line between ---- and ESTAMINET CORNER	

Vol 41

War Diary
of
10th Liverpool R
for period

1st to 31st May
1918

RECONNAISSANCE.

It is considered that the previous reconnoitring and practice was the chief factor that led to coys. reaching their appointed places in good time, and without undue confusion.

Without reconnaissance the forward movement on the morning of the 5th April would have been extremely difficult, and no matter how trying the reconnaissance and practice occupation of positions, I consider the time well spent.

* * * *

D C A Munro, MAJOR,

COMMANDING, 1/10th (SCOTTISH) BATTN. K. L. R.

12th April 1918.

MORALE.

Throughout the whole of the operations the spirits of the men were excellent, despite the fact that they suffered a good deal from cold, especially at nights.

No hot food could be procured, but otherwise rations were plentiful and satisfactory.

Rum arrived in sufficient quantity to allow at least one issue per night.

COMMUNICATIONS.

During the whole of the operations the buried cable from FESTUBERT remained intact, thus giving communication back to Brigade and to units in the rear.

All other lines were broken the first day, and despite many attempts to repair same they never remained intact for more than an hour at a time. This entailed very heavy work for the Runners.

The configuration of the ground did not lend itself very well to the use of visual, and on most days it would have been impossible to see a Heliograph, owing to the mist.

ENEMY TACTICS.

During the period covered, the enemy tactics, apart from his attacks on LAIENS CENTRAL and ROUTE "A" KEEP, were confined to individual sniping and occasional bursts of M.G. fire.

CAPTURES.

The total captures by the Battn:-

Unwounded men. 22.
Wounded men. 6.
Machine guns. 3.

DEFENCES.

The few concrete shelters that there were withstood the bombardments, and had there been more of them the casualties would have been considerably less. In one case, a shell entered obliquely below the shelter, and lifted the floor to the ceiling. In no other instance was a shelter noticed to be damaged.

The other defences were of poor quality, and could not withstand much shelling.

SUGGESTIONS.

It is suggested that concrete shelters should have, in addition, a depth of concrete on the floor. This it is hoped would prevent the recurrence of the above episode.

Rifles, and particularly Lewis Guns, suffered from lack of rifle oil. It is suggested that a supply of rifle oil should be kept in Keeps.

- 3 -

APRIL 14th. contd.
2 coys. and 2 platoons of the 13th Bn.K.L.R.

APRIL 15th.
The relief was complete about 3 a.m., and the dispositions were then as under :-
"X" Coy. in FESTUBERT EAST KEEP and FESTUBERT SUPPORT.
"Y" " in FESTUBERT CENTRAL, and defensive flank (shell hole positions.
"Z" " garrison of CAILLOUX NORTH and SOUTH.
HQ. Details in McMAHON TRENCH and COTTAGES.

The morning was quiet, but FESTUBERT was shelled very heavily the whole of the afternoon with 5.9 and 8" shells.

Officers of 1st Gloucesters and 1st South Wales Borderers (1st Division) came to reconnoitre with a view to relief the following day.

Night passed off fairly quietly, with occasional burst of 77 mm's on TURING FORK Road.

APRIL 16th.
At 9.5 a.m. the enemy commenced to shell heavily the whole of the FESTUBERT LOCALITY. The trenches in FESTUBERT SUPPORT were completely destroyed, and also many fire-bays in FESTUBERT CENTRAL. The bombardment was kept up until 7 p.m. with two short breaks.

Between 4 p.m. and 5 p.m. Lt.Col.T.H.PRICE, D.S.O., G.S.O.1, 55th Division, visited us. He was followed soon after by Major DUNCOMBE, Brigade Major 165 Brigade.

The Battalion was relieved by 3 coys. of the 1st Gloucesters and 1 coy. of S.W.Borderers. The relief was complete about 11.15 p.m.

APRIL 16th.
On relief the Battn. marched by platoons to BEUVRY, and enbussed for billets in RAINBERT, where they arrived about 4 a.m. 16th April, 1918.

o o o o

CASUALTIES. The casualties suffered by the Battn. were :-

Officers.	Killed.	2.
	Wounded.	7.
	" (at duty)	1.
	Missing.	1.
		11.
Other Ranks.	Killed.	49.
	Wounded.	127.
	Missing.	7.
	Died of Wounds.	6.
		189.

TOTAL. 200.

- 2 -

APRIL 10th contd.

2 platoons of the 13th Bn. K.L.R. (3rd Division) were moved up to the BRICK LINE, also 2 platoons of the 1/4th S.Lancs (Pioneers).

1 coy. of the 1/8th S.Lancs. was moved up to support LOISNE CENTRAL.

1 platoon of "V" Coy. was posted in the gun pits immediately West of FESTUBERT.

Enemy aircraft were very active, and aeroplanes, with British markings, dropped bombs about GORRE.

APRIL 11th.

At 7.45 a.m. on the morning of 11th April a hurricane bombardment was opened on TUNING FORK LINE, and was kept up until 8.15 a.m. No enemy attack developed on our sector, and the remainder of the day was comparatively quiet.

About 11.30 p.m. orders were received that the Battn. (less 3 coys.) and 1 coy. of 13th Bn. K.L.R. would relieve the 1/8th Bn. K.L.R. and 2 coys. of the 1/6th Bn. K.L.R. in FESTUBERT. The coy. of the 13th Bn. K.L.R. already in FESTUBERT were ordered to 'stand fast'.

APRIL 12th.

The relief was carried out; and completed by 4 a.m. 12th inst. The Battn. was disposed as follows :-
Hdqrs. in FESTUBERT, near the Cross-roads.
"Y" Coy. in CAILLOUX SOUTH and McMAHON TRENCH.

The remaining coys. of the Battn. retained their former positions, and came under the command of O.C. 13th Bn. K.L.R., with the exception of "Z" Coy. in LOISNE CENTRAL, who came under the command of Major T.M. PILKINGTON, 1/5th S.Lancs Regt.

The 2 coys. and 2 platoons of the 13th Bn. K.L.R. under my command in FESTUBERT occupied positions as under :-
1 coy.   FESTUBERT EAST KEEP, COTTAGES Nos. 1 & 2, and CAILLOUX NORTH KEEP.
1 "   FESTUBERT CENTRAL and SUPPORT.
2 platoons(of third coy.) Shell hole positions, and defensive flank West of CAILLOUX NORTH.

Enemy comparatively quiet during the day, but began shelling heavily after 5 p.m.

Orders were received that "X" Coy (Liverpool Scottish) and "D" Coy. 13th Bn. K.L.R. would make an attack on ROUTE "A" KEEP about midnight. "X" Coy. had for their immediate objective the ruins immediately South of ROUTE "A" KEEP. This they captured, together with 9 prisoners and 1 machine gun. The coy. then moved forward and supported the attack on ROUTE "A" KEEP. The capture was complete by 2 a.m. 13-4-18.

APRIL 13th.

About 4 a.m. I took 2nd Lt. ROWE and 2 Scouts to reconnoitre and find out how the situation stood about ROUTE "A" KEEP. We found Capt.J.R.MacSWINEY in command, and organising the defence of the Keep. Everything being satisfactory we started to come back, and walked into a party of 10 Germans on the road leading from ROUTE "A" KEEP to CAILLOUX. We succeeded in escaping to ROUTE "A" KEEP where we gave the alarm. The enemy counter-attacked almost immediately, but was easily beaten off.

At 7 a.m. a German surrendered to the garrison in CAILLOUX.

The morning was quiet; but FESTUBERT was heavily shelled during the whole of the evening.

At 5.15 p.m. orders were received for the following adjustments. 1/5th S.Lancs. relieving "Z" Coy. in LOISNE CENTRAL, "Z" Coy. proceeded to ROUTE "A" KEEP where they relieved "D" coy. 13th Bn. K.L.R. "X" and "Y" coys. proceeded to FESTUBERT and relieved

........contd.

1/10th (SCOTTISH) BATTN. THE KING'S (L'POOL REGIMENT).

NARRATIVE OF OPERATIONS
from
April 9th to April 15th. 1918.

On April 8th the Battn. was in billets as follows :-
Hdqrs., Transport, "Y" and "Z" Coys. at ESPLANX PARK.
"V" and "X" Coys. at LE HAMEL.

APRIL 9th. At 4.45 a.m. on April 9th orders were received to move to positions in the TUNING FORK LOCALITY. The Battn. moved off by coys. in half-platoons, about 5.30 a.m.

All this time the whole area was being heavily shelled by the enemy, and as gas was being freely used the moving up was rendered very difficult.

Coys. arrived and got into positions in the TUNING FORK LOCALITY about 7 a.m. and were disposed as under :-
3 coys. from TUNING FORK NORTH to LOISNE CENTRAL.
1 coy. in TUNING FORK SWITCH.
Hdqrs. in house where TUNING FORK LINE joins the TUNING FORK NORTH ROAD.

During the whole morning the shelling was intense, and the heavy mist made it almost impossible to see what was taking place. Owing to the heavy shelling, Hdqrs. moved into the trench.

About 12 noon all troops in the TUNING FORK LOCALITY came under the orders of 165 Brigade, and under the immediate orders of Lt. Col. McKRIG, D.S.O., 1/6th Bn. K.L.R.

Owing to the obscurity of the situation on our left flank, I sent 2nd Lt. G.E.ROWE to find out the situation. He came back and reported that Portuguese troops had been firing on him. Not satisfied with the situation, I went out to personally reconnoitre. Finding LOISNE CENTRAL unoccupied, I at once ordered "Z" Coy. to occupy it. This was the more necessary as there was a 6" How. Battery and an 18 pounder Battery immediately in rear of the position, and the Germans were seen about 350 yards away. I came back and reported to Lt. Col. McKRIG what I had done.

About this time we learned that ROUTE "A" KEEP was in the hands of the enemy, but not knowing his strength, and not having sufficient men to risk a counter-attack, he was left in possession.

Battn. Hdqrs. then moved into a concrete dugout occupied by Lt. Col. McKRIG and his Hdqrs.

About 3 p.m. half of "V" Coy. were moved to support "X" Coy. in the TUNING FORK SWITCH.

Towards evening, the shelling died down, and the mist lifted. During the night patrols were sent out to keep in touch with the enemy, and a post was established in the ORCHARD South of ROUTE "A" KEEP to guard the road.

APRIL 10th The morning of the 10th brought little change in the tactical situation.

Two attacks were made by the enemy on LOISNE CENTRAL, the first at 6 a.m. and the second at 10 a.m. These were easily beaten off. The third and more determined attempt was made at dusk. A party of the enemy with machine guns crept up ditch, and attempted to establish themselves behind LOISNE CENTRAL. The party with two machine guns were captured, and many Germans were killed.

NARRATIVE OF OPERATIONS FROM 9/4/18 to 16/4/18.

At 4 a.m. on the 9/4/18 'Z' Coy. moved forward from Reserve and occupied a position at LOISNE CENTRAL. We were heavily shelled the whole morning and in the afternoon the enemy formed up to attack about 1000 yards in front of our positions, but was dispersed with L.G. fire. The following morning he heavily bombarded our line for two hours. About mid-day two enemy M.G. teams had succeeded in working round our right flank and were firing on us from the rear. We immediately sent out a party of men and either killed or took prisoner the two enemy teams. The same night, owing to casualties, I was detailed to report to 'X' Coy.

On the morning of the 11/4/18 I was sent forward to occupy shell hole positions in the orchard which is situated N. of TUNING FORK E. KEEP. The remainder of the day was quiet.

On the 13/4/18 'X' Coy. were ordered to attack and capture a strong point 50 yds S. of ROUTE A KEEP, which they did capturing 10 prisoners and 2 M.Gs.

On the night of the 13/4/18 the company relieved the garrison of FESTUBERT E KEEP, FESTUBERT CENTRAL and SOUTH. We remained here for two days, during which time we were heavily shelled.

On the night of the 16/4/18 we were relieved by a Company of the Gloucester Regt.,

                                          (sd) LAYTON A.DAVEY, 2/Lt.

9/4/18 to 11/4/18 -   13 Platoon 'Z' Coy.
11/4/18 to 16/4/18.   5 & 6 Platoons 'X' Coy.

3/8/18.

RECONNAISSANCE.

It is considered that the previous reconnoitring and practice was the chief factor that led to coys. reaching their appointed places in good time, and without undue confusion.

Without reconnaissance the forward movement on the morning of the 9th April would have been extremely difficult, and no matter how trying the reconnaissance and practice occupation of positions, I consider the time well spent.

(sd) D.C.D.MUNRO, Major,
18th April, 1918.   COMMANDING, 1/10th (SCOTTISH) Battn. K.L.R.

MORALE.

Throughout the whole of the operations the spirits of the men were excellent, despite the fact that they suffered a good deal from cold, especially at nights.

No hot food could be procured, but otherwise rations were plentiful and satisfactory.

Rum arrived in sufficient quantity to allow at least one issue per night.

COMMUNICATIONS.

During the whole of the operations the buried cable from FESTUBERT remained intact, thus giving communication back to Brigade and to units in the rear.

All other lines were broken the first day, and despite many attempts to repair same they never remained intact for more than an hour at a time. This entailed very heavy work for the Runners.

The configuration of the ground did not lend itself very well to the use of visual, and on most days it would have been impossible to see a heliograph, owing to the mist.

ENEMY TACTICS.

During the period covered, the enemy tactics, apart from his attacks on LOISNE CENTRAL and ROUTE A KEEP, were confined to individual sniping and occasional bursts of M.G. fire.

CAPTURES.

The total captures by the Battn:-

Unwounded men.	20.
Wounded men.	5.
Machine guns.	3.

DEFENCES.

The few concrete shelters that there were withstood the bombardments, and had there been more of them the casualties would have been considerably less. In one case, a shell entered obliquely below the shelter, and lifted the floor to the ceiling. In no other instance was a shelter noticed to be damaged.

The other defences were of poor quality, and could not withstand much shelling.

SUGGESTIONS.

It is suggested that concrete shelters should have, in addition, a depth of concrete on the floor. This it is hoped would prevent the recurrence of the above episode.

Rifles and particularly Lewis guns, suffered from lack of rifle oil. It is suggested that a supply of rifle oil should be kept in Keeps.

- 3 -

APRIL 14th.

The relief was complete about 5 a.m., and the dispositions were then as under :-
- "X" Coy. in FESTUBERT EAST KEEP and FESTUBERT SUPPORT.
- "V" Coy. in FESTUBERT CENTRAL, and defensive flank (shell hole positions.
- "Y" Coy. garrison of CAILLOUX NORTH AND SOUTH.
- H.Q. details in McMAHON TRENCH and COTTAGES.

The morning was quiet, but FESTUBERT was shelled very heavily the whole of the afternoon with 5.9 and 8" shells.

Officers of 1st Gloucesters and 1st South Wales Borderers (1st Division) came to reconnoitre with a view to relief the following day.

Night passed off fairly quickly, with occasional burst of 77 mm's on TUNING FORK Road.

APRIL 15th.

At 9.5 a.m. the enemy commenced to shell heavily the whole of the FESTUBERT LOCALITY. The trenches in FESTUBERT SUPPORT were completely destroyed, and also many fire bays in FESTUBERT CENTRAL. The bombardment was kept up until 7 p.m. with two short breaks.

Between 4 p.m. and 5 p.m. Lt.Col.T.R.PRICE, D.S.O., G.S.O.I, 55th Division, visited us. He was followed soon after by Major DUNCOMBE, Brigade Major, 165 Brigade.

The Battalion was relieved by two Coys. of the 1st Gloucesters and 1 coy. of S.W.Borderers. The relief was complete about 11.15 p.m.

APRIL 16th.

On relief the Battn. marched by platoons to BEUVRY, and embussed for billets in RAIMBERT, where they arrived about 4 a.m. 16th April, 1918.

* * * * * * *

CASUALTIES.   The casualties suffered by the Battn: were :-

Officers.	Killed.	2	
	Wounded.	7	
	"(at duty)	1	
	missing.	1	
			11
Other Ranks.	Killed.	49	
	Wounded.	127	
	Missing.	7	
	Died of Wounds.	6	
			189

TOTAL. 200.

– 2 –

APRIL 10th. contd.

2 Platoons of the 13th Bn. K.L.R. (3rd Division) were moved up to the SWITCH LINE, also 2 platoons of the 1/4th S.Lancs. (Pioneers).

1 Coy. of the 1/5th S.Lancs. was moved up to support LOISNE CENTRAL.

1 platoon of "V" Coy. was posted in the gun pits immediately west of FESTUBERT.

Enemy aircraft were very active, and aeroplanes, with British markings, dropped bombs about GORRE.

APRIL 11th.

At 7.45 a.m. on the morning of 11th April a hurricane bombardment was opened on TUNING FORK LINE, and was kept up until 8.15 a.m. No enemy attack developed on our sector, and the remainder of the day was comparatively quiet.

About 11.30 p.m. orders were received that the Battn. (less 3 coys.) and 1 coy. of 13th Bn.K.L.R. would relieve the 1/5th Bn.K.L.R. and 2 Coys. of the 1/6th Bn.K.L.R. in FESTUBERT. The Coy. of the 13th Bn.K.L.R. already in FESTUBERT were ordered to 'stand fast'.

APRIL 12th.

The relief was carried out; and completed by 4 a.m. 12th inst. The Battn. was disposed as follows :-
Hdqrs. in FESTUBERT, near the Cross-roads.
"Y" Coy. in CAILLOUX SOUTH and McMAHON TRENCH.
The remaining Coys. of the Battn. retained their former positions, and came under the command of O.C., 13th Bn.K.L.R. with the exception of "Z" Coy. in LOISNE CENTRAL who came under the command of Major W.M.PILKINGTON, 1/5th S.Lancs.Regt.

The 2 Coys. and 2 platoons of the 13th Bn. K.L.R. under my command in FESTUBERT occupied positions as under :-
1 Coy. FESTUBERT EAST KEEP, COTTAGES Nos. 1 & 2, and
   CAILLOUX NORTH KEEP.
1 " FESTUBERT CENTRAL & SUPPORT.
2 platoons (of third Coy). shell hole positions, and
   defensive flank West of CAILLOUX NORTH.

Enemy comparatively quiet during the day, but began shelling heavily after 5 p.m.

Orders were received that "X" Coy. (Liverpool Scottish) and "D" Coy. 13th Bn.K.L.R. would make an attack on ROUTE A KEEP about midnight. "X" Coy. had for their immediate objective the ruins immediately South of ROUTE A KEEP. This they captured, together with 9 prisoners and 1 machine gun. The Coy. then moved forward and supported the attack on ROUTE A KEEP The capture was complete by 2 a.m. 13-4-18.

APRIL 13th.

About 4.a.m. I took 2/Lieut. ROME and 2 Scouts to reconnoitre and find out how the situation stood about ROUTE A KEEP. We found Capt.J.R.MacSWINEY in command, and organising the defence of the Keep. Everything being satisfactory we started to come back and walked into a party of 10 Germans on the road leading from ROUTE A KEEP to CAILLOUX. We succeeded in escaping to ROUTE A KEEP where we gave the alarm. The enemy counter-attacked almost immediately, but was easily beaten off.

At 7 a.m. a German surrendered to the garrison in CAILLOUX.

The morning was quiet, but FESTUBERT was heavily shelled during the whole of the evening.

At 9.15 p.m. orders were received for the following adjustments. 1/5th S.Lancs. relieving "Z" Coy. in LOISNE CENTRAL, "Z" Coy. proceeded to ROUTE A KEEP where they relieved 'D' Coy. 13th Bn. K.L.R. "X" and "V" Coys. proceeded to FESTUBERT and relieved 2 coys. and 2 platoons of the 13th Bn. K.L.R.

1/10th (SCOTTISH) BATTN. THE KING'S (L'POOL REGIMENT).

NARRATIVE OF OPERATIONS.

from

April 9th to April 15th, 1918.

On April 8th the Battn. was in billets as follows :-
Hdqrs., Transport, "Y" and "Z" Coys. at MESPLAUX FARM. "V" and "X" Coys. at LE HAMEL.

APRIL 9th. At 4.45 a.m. on April 9th orders were received to move to positions in the TUNING FORK LOCALITY. The Battn. moved off by Coys. in half platoons, about 5.30 a.m.

All this time the whole area was being heavily shelled by the enemy, and as gas was being freely used the moving up was rendered very difficult.

Coys. arrived and got into positions in the TUNING FORK LOCALITY about 7 a.m. and were disposed as under :-
3 Coys. from TUNING FORK NORTH to LOISNE CENTRAL.
1 Coy. in TUNING FORK SWITCH.
Hdqrs. in house where TUNING FORK LINE joins the TUNING FORK NORTH ROAD.

During the whole morning the shelling was intense, and the heavy mist made it almost impossible to see what was taking place. Owing to the heavy shelling, Hdqrs. moved into the trench.

About 12 noon all troops in the TUNING FORK LOCALITY came under the orders of 165th Brigade, and under the immediate orders of Lt.Col.McKAIG, D.S.O., 1/6th Bn.K.L.R.

Owing to the obscurity of the situation on our left flank, I sent 2/Lieut. C.E.ROME to find out the situation. He came back and reported that Portuguese troops had been firing on him. Not satisfied with the situation, I went out to personally reconnoitre. Finding LOISNE CENTRAL unoccupied, I at once ordered "Z" Coy. to occupy it. This was the more necessary as there was a 6" How. battery and an 18 pdr. battery immediately in rear of the position, and the Germans were seen about 350 yards away. I came back and reported to Lt.Col. McKAIG what I had done.

About this time we learned that ROUTE A KEEP was in the hands of the enemy, but not knowing his strength, and not having sufficient men to risk a counter-attack he was left in possession.

Battn. Hdqrs. then moved into a concrete dugout occupied by Lt.Col.McKAIG and his Hdqrs.

About 3 p.m. half of 'V' Coy. were moved to support 'X' Coy. in the TUNING FORK SWITCH.

Towards evening, the shelling died down, and the mist lifted. During the night patrols were sent out to keep in touch with the enemy, and a post was established in the ORCHARD south of ROUTE A KEEP to guard the road.

APRIL 10th. The morning of the 10th brought little change in the tactical situation.

Two attacks were made by the enemy on LOISNE CENTRAL, the first at 6 a.m. and the second at 10 a.m. These were easily beaten off. The third and more determined attempt was made at dusk. A party of the enemy with machine guns crept up ditch, and attempted to establish themselves behind LOISNE CENTRAL. The party with two machine guns were captured, and many Germans were killed.

REPORT
ON
COUNTER-ATTACK DELIVERED AGAINST ROUTE "A" KEEP
by
"X" Coy. 13th Battn. K.L.R. and "X" Coy. 1/10th (SCOTTISH) Bn. K.L.R.

Reference Map COMBE 1/ST@DC.

Acting on instructions of the Commanding Officer, 13th Bn. K.L.R. (attached) my Coy. assembled at point ordered, at 11 p.m. 13-4-18.

As soon as the barrage opened, my Coy. moved forward as quickly as possible extending to 2 paces, at approximately 80 yards from our objective (M.G. in ruins at X.29.b.25.50).

When the barrage lifted, I was about 30 yards away from the ruins. My coy. at once rushed in, taking the enemy completely by surprise. 5 of the Gun team were killed; the remaining 9 offered no resistance, and were taken prisoners.

My casualties were 1 man slightly wounded by M.G. fire.

About 12.10 a.m. I had placed my Coy. into a defensive position, and awaited information from ROUTE "A" KEEP, as ordered.

Fighting went on in the KEEP until 1.30 a.m. when, having received no message from the 13th Bn.K.L.R., I went forward to reconnoitre. I found that both their Officers were casualties, and that they were only in possession of the Southern end of the KEEP. They had run out of bombs, and were in a disorganised condition.

At this point, I took charge, and brought forward 4 boxes of bombs, which I had in reserve, and issued them to the forward blocks, with instructions to hold on until further supplies could be obtained. A party of 1 N.C.O. and 10 O.R's were despatched to the TUNING FORK "A" KEEP toobtain as many bombs as possible.

The situation was reported to the Commanding Officer, 13th Battn. K.L.R. by wire and runner, asking for more bombs.

At approximately 2.30 a.m., having obtained 7 more boxes of bombs, I organised several bombing parties of 1 N.C.O. and 5 O.R's, sending them forward up various trenches, followed by another party of 6 O.R's to be posted at dug-out entrances, and at intervals along the trench. These parties met with very little resistance, and had cleared the enemy out of the whole system by 3.30 a.m.

The Coy. was then re-organised, and the trenches manned.

A feeble attempt to re-enter the KEEP was made from the Eastern flank at about 4.45 a.m. This was dispersed by M.G. fire.

I then handed over to 2 Officers of 13th Bn. L.L.R. who had been sent as reinforcements.

* * * *

The following N.C.O's and men of my coy. distinguished themselves during the attack.

    335172 Sgt. F. J. CRANE, M.M.
    335807 " J. SCARISBRICK.
    335414 Cpl. G. JORDAN.
    335253 Pte. T. WEEVERS.

         (sgd) J. R. MacS"IVEN, Captain.
       O.C. "X" Coy, 1/10th (SCOTTISH) Battn. K.L.R.

14th April 1918.

- 2 -

order, thank goodness, and I myself think that the feeding of the Company (I suppose it was the same throughout the Battn) was absolutely wonderful 35 to 40 bags of food each night. More power to the transport and our irresistable C.Q.M.S. (a lad named BENSON) The sport was good now for the Huns were wandering aimlessly about in droves or herds (I think pigs walk in herds) and our Lewis guns and rifles were in perfect order so it was great. The prisoners we took all gave themselves up said they were of the 4th Ersatz Division and just come from Russian "Tres bon" Russia they said. That accounted for their walking about I suppose. Well to exaggerate a little each bay were knee deep in empties and it took me all my time getting S.A.A. and bombs from the rear (getting the men for the carrying I mean). The old Hun turned nasty again about the 4th day and I think the old Pork and Beans must have left the Breech blocks in the guns for he suddenly started firing point blank at us at about 500 yards range. Phew that was too bad. We established our Coy. H.Qrs. in the concrete dugout and got on alright from the tout suite gun. The men had to dig in just behind LOISNE CENTRAL so they, too, were alright. Some of our guns were ranging now to our delight and one day, I forget which, we gave him hell and scattered the infantry (who were still wandering round only our fellows were tired of mowing them down) with every round. Their target seemed to be a large farm on our left front and the shooting was perfect. Things were straightening themselves now and we had listening posts and patrols out each night. It was getting quite a good war again when on the afternoon of the 5th day, a large party attempted to raid us and take the farm buildings behind us. Luckily we were ready although he got in between us and 'Y' Coy. on our right. After a few curtains of M.G. Bullets over our trench he dashed forward but at the same time we were ready and got him fair and square. After some hand to hand work which lasted only a few minutes we counted up. I counted 25 dead and wounded lying wet through in the ditch between the TUNING FORK and LOISNE CENTRAL and 19 prisoners were sent to the rear. Poor fellows, they must have had a rough time of it, all seemed to be demoralised. Things went quiet again except the H.V. gun and on the night of the 6th day were relieved from the position by a Company of the 5th South Lancs. and ordered up to the newly recaptured place ROUTE A KEEP. We had heard about this place before and wern't particularly keen to dash up there. However it had to be done, so we stole off a very much battered crew then but as long as the food kept good and Jerry we didn't mind. We took over from the 13th King's who seemed to be on the verge of collapse when we got there. They fled like rabbits when they saw us in the trench. What a desolate place ROUTE A was that night. Dead of both sides lying all about. Reminded me of the Crater at HOOGE. An awful place, absolutely no movement whatever by day and hold on at all costs was the order given. The rations and rum (God bless the Q.M.) were issued by night and barring an eagle eye watch by day nothing happened at all. Well our Coy. were lucky for during the two days we were in ROUTE A he never bothered us except for an awful rattle of M.G. bullets just on the Stand To in the evening. To cover the advance of his night forward posts I fancy. Things went on alright, the O.C., Coy. and the two remaining officers, Messrs KELLIE and PRICE (both since killed poor chaps) nearly yelled with joy when we heard that the 1st Bn. of the S.W.B. would relieve us that night and that we were going down the line. The relief came up well to time and off we go in little detachments through the ruins of poor old GORRE, LE QUESNOY and BEUVRY and hopped on to motor busses on the BETHUNE ROAD, and off we went to RAIMBERT for what I considered a well earned rest.

I heard afterwards that Jerry came over next morning and took ROUTE A KEEP off the S.W.B. Lucky 'Z' Coy.).

(sd) JAS. BRIGGS, Sergt.
during the stunt
C.S.M. of 'Z' Coy.

April 9th to April 16th.

MESPLAUX FARM TO RAIMBERT.

At about 3.30 a.m. on the morning of April 9th I was awakened by the explosion of large high explosive shells which seemed to be dropping a good sight nearer the farm than they ever dropped before. I just hopped downstairs and found the yard in a state of excitement, and could hear a well known phrase coming from the direction of the Orderly Room "Stand To". Well the thundering of the guns was by this time increasing and I just said to myself that "old Jerry was going to attack". As events turned out and before the 9th April was through I found that my assertions were not far wrong. After about 20 minutes there stood 'Z' Coy. of the 1/10th (Scottish) K.L.R. on the road outside the Farm shivering in the mist and cursing and swearing the while which increased fourfold as I slung the extra bandolier to each man. The bedlam in the Farmyard was still going on and after I had got our Company Lewis gun limber at the rear of the Company I reported "Ready to Move" to my very cool and collected Company Officer. The C.O., gave him the word to get to his 'BUSTLE' position tout suite so off we go, I'm afraid with wind vertical. The gunfire was at this point awful the whole front was ablaze with the flashes of the Huns artillery. We hadn't got more than 200 yards along the road before the two scouts which the O.C., Coy. had pushed forward reported that to get along that road was suicide. About turn was given so back we go past the farm again to go on out towards LE HAMEL. Getting across there was bad going owing to the mist, the LOISNE stream and several successive belts of wire which ran across towards LOCON. To make things worse the whiff of gas was getting stronger each pace so of course we had to don our masks which do not tend to make marching all clover. On we pushed, great H.E. shells and gas as well dropping all around us up to LOISNE CHATEAU. Here we picked up spades and picks and then plodded on. How the platoons (we split up here and marched at 100 yards interval) missed getting wiped out between LOISNE CHATEAU and the TUNING FORK LINE goodness only knows. However our first casualty was just getting into the trench, a chap hit in the neck, not too bad. He is having a great time in NOTTINGHAM at present. Well from then (it was about 5.30 a.m.) until about 4 in the afternoon, that old TUNING FORK LINE was an inferno. Naturally our casualties were severe but the boys who were left were by this time hardened to it and gave a Bosche airman (who tried to rattle us with M.G. bullets about 2 p.m.) a hell of a pasting. He retired dam smart anyhow. Hunger prevailed about now and after consultation with the O.C., Coy. I sent a Corpl. and a couple of men with a chit to LOISNE CHATEAU and nearly went into a fit of delight when they returned later with a tin of biscuits and 2 boxes of bully. Here we found through our C.O., that our left which should I believe have been occupied by the 5th King's Own were out of touch with us and I afterwards heard that about 20 artillerymen held the LOISNE CENTRAL TRENCH during the strafe of the day. Very good that. At nightfall our Coy. were pushed over to the left and took over LOISNE CENTRAL which was then vacant. That started it. The Coy. H.Qrs. were in the gunpits and a concrete dugout behind. The night passed quite uneventful except that a very smart looking young German came over and gave himself up to us. At 'Stand To' the following morning the O.C., Coy. and I had a tour of inspection looking at the wire and the trench in general. His snipers which were hard to locate were very troublesome and about 6 a.m. on the morning of the 10th Capt. MACKAY, a gentleman and a soldier, was killed, dead loss to us. 2/Lieut T.W.PILKINGTON assumed command of the Coy. (one of the best, gone to the Yanks, now worse luck). The rations arrived in good

- 2 -

On the night of the 12th/13th our company was relieved by the 1/5th South Lancashires and we proceeded to ROUTE A KEEP where we relieved the 13th K.L.R. and held the Keep for 48 hours without incident except for intermittent shelling.

On the night of the 14th/15th we were relieved by the 2nd S.W.B. and proceeded down the line for a short rest.

(sd) 356539. R.J.H.BELL, Sgt.
'Z' Coy.
1/10th Battn. (Scottish) K.L.R.

Narrative of tour in the Line.

From April 9th - 16th, 1918.

Sgt. BELL.
'Z' Coy.
1/10th (Scottish) K.L.R.

In the early hours of the morning of the 9th April while occupying rest billets at MESPLAUX FARM the Battalion received orders to "stand to". My company leaving MESPLAUX about 4 a.m. proceeded via LE HAMEL and GORRE to our appointed positions in the NORTH TUNING FORK LINE, detaching a party at GORRE, which was heavily shelled to bring up the Lewis guns, picks, spades and ammunition. These were successfully brought up after a slight delay. All this time the enemy barrage continued in intensity, a large percentage of gas shells being used, until about 12 noon when a considerable reduction was noted. Every man was on the 'qui vive' and special anxiety was noticeable during the early hours because of the mist which hung about making observation very difficult. Our anxiety was unnecessary for the battalion in front of us effectively smashed the German attacks. Now during this time it must not be thought we got off scot free, our casualties were fairly heavy, nearly all of them /occupying the line, very few being hit on the way up.

/occurring
whilst

The afternoon of the 9th was fairly quiet and about 5 p.m. that night our C.O., came along and ordered us to move to the left to LOISNE CENTRAL to help to cover the division's flank which had been left open by the retirement of the Portuguese troops on our left.

Immediately on occupying our position a German was captured on the wire in our front.

During the whole of the day a noticeable feature of the attack was the effective way in which our guns were silenced.

The night of the 9th/10th passed very quietly but when dawn broke on the morning of the 10th large numbers of the enemy were seen moving forward presumably to the attack. At once a heavy rifle and Lewis gun fire was directed on the advancing Bosche who was trying to work forward on our front and flank, and with such good effect that he was checked while still 600 yards away, when we proceeded to dig in, notwithstanding our harassing fire. After a short time all movement of the enemy ceased and we settled down to being intermittently shelled during which time we had several casualties including our O.C., Coy.

About 5 p.m. that night a party of the enemy worked up a ditch on our right and succeeded in occupying LOISNE FARM in our rear, with about 30 men and 2 machine guns. A small party of our company and a platoon of the 1/5th South Lancashires at once attacked the farm killed many of the enemy captured the two machine guns and took sixteen prisoners.

During the night of the 10th/11th a patrol of 1 officer and 6 other ranks reconnoitred a trench running due north to the enemy's lines but found it unoccupied. The remainder of the night passed without event.

In the course of the night of the 11th/12th three of the enemy blundered on to our wire, and after we had challenged one of our Lewis guns opened fire. The enemy at once turned about leaving one of their number wounded who however died soon after. Again the remainder of the night and the next day the 12th passed without incident.

Everything was quiet that day and we were relieved the night of the 14th/15th by a Coy. of the 1/5th South Lancs. and went up to the newly taken ROUTE A KEEP. During all this time and up to the time of being relieved we had champion rations thanks to the good work done by our C.Q.M.S. and transport. ROUTE A KEEP turned out to be not quite so bad as we expected but it was not a very nice place to live. The night of the 16th/17th we were relieved by a Coy. of the 1st S.W.Bs. and went down the line on a well earned rest, but we did not get a very long one.

                                        (sd) ALBERT STANLEY Sergt.,
                                            'Z' Coy. 1/10 K.L.R.

April 9th to 16th.

The Battalion were in reserve at MESPLAUX FARM and on the morning of the 9th of April I had a very rude awakening by the bursting of heavy shells in close proximity to the farm. This would be about 3 a.m. About 10 minutes later the expected order came along "stand-to" needless to say most of the men were already up and dressed so we were soon out on the road and ready to move off extra S.A.A. having been given to everyone in the meantime. Orders came along to get to the 'BUSTLE' positions (TUNING FORK N.) so away we go across country to LE HAMEL and along Short Road. About 100 yards from the cross-roads outside the village of LOISNE here we were split up into parties most of them going along the road towards GORRE so as to pick up Lewis Guns S.A.A. etc., By this time everyone knew that this 'BUSTLE' was not a case of getting in the positions and waiting to go back to breakfast same as previous ones. 2/Lieut. PILKINGTON took command of the parties that went round through GORRE. The remainder went with Capt. McKAY including your humble. At this time we put our S.B.Rs. on also the mist was very thick. Whether it was due to the mist or wearing S.B.Rs. I cannot say but we went too far up the road that runs from LOISNE to FESTUBERT and got lost for a bit. However we soon put that right by Captain Mc.KAY and myself going out and finding our position. We got our people in and found that Mr. PILKINGTON's party was already in position. The first thing that was needed in the trench was more S.A.A. so we got some up from the dump and then it was a case of watching and waiting as we were having a very rough time of it with his bombardment which he kept up all the time till about 2.30 pm when it lifted off us. About 4 p.m. we were moved over to our left and took up a position that should have been occupied by another Battalion, but had not been so, LOISNE CENTRAL where it seemed very quiet and nothing happened much only a bit of rifle practise for us as plenty of Jerries were roaming round in front of us and on our left flank. That night I with three men and my officer done about four hours patrol but gained no information the only thing we heard was plenty of them shouting to one another as if they were lost. Next morning the 10th a great deal of movement was seen in front of us and he tried to get round our left flank but I am rather afraid he regretted this movement as we had plenty of rifle practise and in my bay we were knee deep in empty cases (cartridge) and nl heard afterwards each Lewis gun fired about 2000 rds per gun. About this time we lost our Coy. Commander Capt. McKAY M.C., and 2/Lieut. PILKINGTON took command of the Coy. Next day 11th he succeeded in getting through a gap that was between us and our right 'Y' Coy, but he was quickly ejected by us with the timely help of a party of South Lancs. leaving plenty of dead and about 20 prisoners. We were very much troubled by a gun about this time that was firing at us at point blank range and what I took to be one of our own 18 pdrs that the Pork and Beans had left behind them and of course every time he hit the breastwork it brought the whole bay down so we dug a trench behind this breastwork about 2 feet wide and 5 feet deep and his tout-suite gun as we named it, did not trouble us very much afterwards.

The night of the 12th and 13th a patrol of the enemy got up to our wire and one of our posts succeeded in wounding one of them and myself and another man went out and brought him in. He was questioned by one of our officers and gave information that his regiment was going to attack us at dawn so we got in communication with the heavies and at dawn that morning he got it in the neck what with heavies and Lewis guns and rifle fire result no attack that morning.

Happenings on the 9/4/18.

On the morning of the 9/4/18 'V' Coy. were rushed up to support the 165th Brigade and got into position in the TUNING FORK LINE, being under very heavy shell fire and gas. The right half coy. which I was attached to, had a stretch of trench about 200 yards to man but when we got there we found the trench full of men of the 1/6th K.L.R. However we squeezed in and remained there about two hours and got the Lewis guns into position and everybody loaded up. The right half Coy. then got orders to take up another position about 500 yards on the right but in the same trench, we remainder there about an hour and orders came through to move back to their original position, they remained in that position until about 5 p.m. during which time we had been subjected to heavy shelling fire and gas shells, which caused a great number of casualties, among them being the O.C., Coy. and the Right half company Commander. At 5 p.m. the right half coy. moved up to reinforce 'X' Coy. who were about 600 yards in advance of 'V'. I then joined the left half coy. who had had about 90% of their N.C.Os. knocked out and remained in the TUNING FORK LINE the rest of the day.

(sd). Sgt. J. WREN,
'V' Coy.

On April 9th 'V' Company moved forward and took up a position in the TUNING FORK LINE on the North side of the NORTH TUNING FORK ROAD. In the afternoon of the same day I was sent to reinforce 'X' Company in the TUNING FORK SWITCH LINE with the right half company. I remained here until the night of April 10th when I was moved to the house named "Rest and be thankful" on the North TUNING FORK ROAD. There I had two Lewis gun posts facing North towards the new German line. On the night of the 12th/13th I moved forward into FESTUBERT occupying a shell hole position west of CAILLOUX KEEP facing North. There I remained until the night 16th/17th April when we were relieved by the 1st Division. During this time in the line the half company was subjected to very heavy shelling, but wer engaged in no infantry action.

2nd August, 1918.
(sd) LESTER SHAW, Sec.Lieut.
O.C., No. 1 Platoon.

Report on taking of ROUTE A KEEP.
================================

On the night of the 23rd/24th 'X' Company plus 1 platoon of 'Z' Coy. were detailed to attack and take ROUTE A KEEP. 3.30 a.m. 24/4/18 the five platoons were in position 150 yds in front of enemy, facing North. At 3.55 a.m. our heavies and 18 pdrs assisted by machine gun fire, bombarded position from X.29.b.25.60. to X.29.b.80.60. At 4 a.m. the heavies lifted to the KEEP, and my men moved forward. At 4.5 a.m. the 18 pdrs lifted to the KEEP and my men attacked position between X.29.b.25.60. and X.29.b.80.60. taking a machine gun and killing five which were acting as covering party for enemy wiring party. At 4.7 a.m. barrage lifted to a line from X.23.d.30.30. to X.29.b.90.90. My men then went forward with great dash and took the KEEP including three more M.Gs. and 10 prisoners. During this time we had suffered approximately 50 casualties. They were at once organised and prepared for a counter attack, but the only thing seen of the enemy was him running in the opposite direction. One of his own M.Gs. were placed in position and fired upon the retreating enemy. Throughout the remainder of the day we were heavily shelled, and lost a further 20 casualties slightly wounded. About midnight the enemy heavily bombarded the KEEP but no further casualties occurred and no infantry action followed. At 1 a.m. 25/4/18 I handed over ROUTE A KEEP to 'D' Coy. of the 2/10th K.L.R. I returned with approximately 60 O.Rs.

1/8/18.
(sd) LAYTON. A. DAVEY, 2/Lt.

Narrative of Operations of 'Y' Company from 9th to 16th
April 1918.
================================

On the morning of 9th April the Battn. was in rest billets in MESPLAUX FARM. At 4 a.m. 'Y' Coy. received the order to "stand to" and about 5 a.m. were ordered to proceed to 'BUSTEE' positions.

Route taken by the Coy. was through LE HAMEL to GORRE, thence by track in front of GORRE CHATEAU to TUNING FORK handle, TUNING FORK NORTH ROAD to the TUNING FORK SWITCH arriving about 6.30 a.m. There was a very thick fog and a good deal of shelling on all roads and tracks and trenches.

At 3 p.m. we received orders to take up position up in TUNING FORK LINE on the left of ROUTE 20. We were in position about 7 p.m. The night was quiet.

10th. Morning. Heavy shelling of Coy. sector. Had some good shooting by Lewis guns and rifles at Bosche round ROUTE A KEEP. In the afternoon about 50 Bosche attacked Coy. on our left in LOISNE CENTRAL some good shooting by Lewis gun on left of Coy. front; attack broken up and some prisoners taken. Another quiet night.

April 11th. Continuous shelling on position all day relieved by 1/6th K.L.R. at 11 p.m. to take over CAILLOUX KEEP and McMAHON POST. This was complete by 5 a.m. two platoons attached to Coy. from 13th K.L.R. took up shell hole position on left flank.

12th. Two platoons of 13th K.L.R. relieved by two platoons of 'V' Coy.

13th to 16th. Nothing of interest except a few low flying H.A. to try to locate our line.

16th/17th. Relieved by 1st Gloucesters and proceeded to REIMBART.

(sd) S.R.LEWIS, Capt.
O.C. 'Y' Coy. during operations.

1/8/18.

"Y" Coy.   12 Platoon.

Apl. 9th to Apl 15th Operations.

We were stationed at MESPLAUX FARM, near LOCON on April 8th.

At about 4 a.m. on April 9th we were wakened by the noise of heavy shelling and a few minutes after we received the order "Stand to". We paraded battle order and marched off by half companies. Capt. (then Lieut.) LEWIS was in temporary command of 'Y' Company and Lieut. HUGHES was in command of the left half of the Company. Shortly after leaving the farm we came under heavy shell fire and the half company divided into two parties (roughly two platoons). Instead of keeping to the road we went across a ploughed field. This undoubtedly saved us many casualties as the road was being heavily shelled a little further on. We had a number of casualties on the way up to our position but considering the heavy shelling through which we passed our losses were not so heavy as one would have expected. Once or twice we had to put on our gas masks as the enemy was using gas shells. We experienced a little difficulty in finding our way through the mist etc., but my party (lead by Mr.HUGHES and Sgt. CONNOR) eventually reached the TUNING FORK SWITCH LINE near the North T.F.Road where we took up fire positions. As bullets were passing over our heads we expected to be attacked very soon. Mr. HUGHES and Mr.ARBUCKLE gave orders for every man to slightly oil his bolt and to get ready for the enemy attack. I may say that we were nearly exhausted on arrival at our position. We had walked a considerable distance with gas masks on. An hour or two later the Coy. Lewis gun N.C.O. informed us that the L.G. limber was on the road, near by and we immediately secured our L.Gun and ammunition. After we had got the gun ready for action, we kept in the trench, expecting to see the Germans appear in the distance. We were heavily shelled until about 4 p.m. when the bombardment died down a little. In the evening we joined the remainder of the Coy. in the TUNING FORK LINE in rear of the position we then occupied. My platoon was on the extreme left of the Coy. On our left was a gap of about 300 yards and then 'Z' Coy. Immediately in front of us at a distance of 500 to 600 yards we could see Germans moving about, with full pack on. At one part, there appeared to be no trench. Looking through binoculars we could see odd Germans walking past this gap and then dropping into a trench. We were sniping at them continually and I believe we hit a few. When a group of the enemy went by we fired with the Lewis gun. One of our shells burst in our right front and as the smoke rose we observed Germans running in all directions. We fired into them with rifles and the Lewis gun. On the left 'Z' Coy. we saw a party of the enemy emerge from a gully or sunken road and attack a farm house, on April 10th. We opened cross fire with rifles and the Lewis gun and the officer sent a runner to ascertain the situation. From our position we saw the attack repulsed and as the enemy retired we opened fire on him. About the night of the 11th April we left the TUNING FORK LINE and part of my platoon relieved the 6th Bn. King's (Liverpool Regt.) in Mc.MAHON TRENCH. and the other part went into CAILLOUE KEEP. During the two days and nights we were in McMAHON TRENCH there was no encounter with the enemy. We were then relieved from McMAHON TRENCH by the H.Q., men and proceeded to join our Coy. in CAILLOUX N. Although we were always expecting an attack from the North we were not attacked and on the night of Apl.15 were relieved by the Gloucesters.

(sd) R.H.ROBERTS, Cpl.
'Y' Coy. 12 Platoon.
1/8/18.

On the morning of 9th April 1918 we were suddenly aroused and told to "stand to" because the Germans had started to attack. We had our Battle Order all ready and so we were not long before we were outside ready to move off. While the Platoon roll was being called, one or two big shells came over, and of course we came to the conclusion that something unusual was happening. It did not take us long to move off, but when we got on the roads we found that they were being shelled pretty heavily especially at Cross roads, so the Company promptly got into Artillery formation and started to move towards the line, going across the fields. On the way up we had a few casualties including my senior platoon sergeant, who I bandaged up and left to go to the Dressing Station. The Platoon officer led the way and i brought up the rear of the platoon. When we got back on the roads again, we moved forward in platoons at intervals of 200 yards, roughly between each other, with two connecting files between each platoon. Nearly all the way we had to wear our gas helmets, because there were a big lot of tear gas shells being thrown over at us. When we were going up the TUNING FORK ROAD the two connecting files from our platoon, who were keeping touch with the platoon in front of us, got lost and suddenly we found ourselves on the top of a small trench (or keep) that was being held by the 6th K.L.R. The shelling was very heavy at this period and so the platoon officer decided to attach ourselves to the 6th King's till the shelling had quietened down a bit. So we got into the trench and stayed there for a while, having to wear our gas helmets almost all the time. While we were in this trench I thought of the 26 eggs we had bought the night previous and which would be gone by now. After we had stayed in this trench for a while a runner and a scout were sent out by the Platoon Officer to find out where the rest of the Company were. They came back and told us they knew where the rest of the Company were. So we promptly started to leave the trench and make for the Company in two parties, the officer taking charge of one and myself the other. We found the rest of the Coy. and immediately reported to Coy. H.Qrs. After we found the Coy. we left the part of the trench we had been holding and moved to another part of the line. While we were there the shelling was pretty heavy and there seemed to be some big shells being fired at us from our left rear (LOCON district). We saw plenty of Germans moving about while we were in the line and we kept firing at them and at times we could see them running, which told us our shots were going near the enemy. Up to this time there had been a big lot of casualties in the platoon, my Lewis gun team being all wounded and killed, excepting the N.C.O. in charge. At night we buried the men who were killed in the trench, also some men from other units which had been left in and out of the trench. The next day, things were just about the same, shelling etc, and we had a few more casualties. On the morning of the 11th I was trying to boil some water to make some tea when suddenly a terrific bombardment opened time being 8 a.m. It lasted for 20 minutes and we thought that perhaps the Germans were going to make a daylight raid, but nothing happened. A good job for somebody. The day passed with our lads firing at the Germans who we saw running occasionally across our front. They were roughly about 600 yards away. The night passed with nothing unusual happening. We sent out Scouts in front and there was a party wiring. On the night of the 12th we were relieved from the TUNING FORK LINE by the 6th K.L.R. We went to CAILLOUX KEEP where we relieved the 13th K.L.R. Things were not so bad in CAILLOUX KEEP as they were in the TUNING FORK LINE. We had a pretty fair time while we were in this position

Experiences of 10 Platoon on 9th April 1918.

Arriving at MAPLAQUET FARM on the evening of the 8th April we were told that we were "standing to" ready to move at half an hours notice. We bedded down little dreaming or as a matter of fact caring, that we were right in the shadow of one of the great German efforts to break through. It would be sometime about 4 a.m. when we were roused and ordered to get dressed and "fall in" in battle order, which I should think we accomplished in record time, as from the terrific noise of cannon fire going on we were at once aware "that all was not well". We left our parade ground about 4.30 a.m. led by Mr.MONKHOUSE and had hardly got clear of the precincts of the farm before shells commenced to improve the marching capabilities of us all. When approaching the bend of the road immediately in rear of the farm en route for HAMEL a limber which was a few hundred yards in front was relieved of its means of progression by a shell. Fortunately for us our officer and sergeant decided to cut the corner off by crossing the fields - deep sighs of relief. We arrived at LE HAMEL but luckily this place was not receiving much attention whilst passing through, but evidence was not lacking that it had done. On approaching LOISNE CHATEAU, things became a bit warmer, especially gas shells which necessitated our putting gas masks on. There guiding the platoon in stood our R.S.M. like the proverbial cucumber. Up to now despite the heavy barrage prevailing, our casualties had been very slight, but now things became tropical and having left the road by the Chateau we advanced about 1000 yards and entered a trench unoccupied with the exception of about two sections belonging to other units. Here we were ordered into the trench as the enemy had come right down behind us on the sector on our left and it was absolutely essential that this trench should be occupied to prevent the enemy enveloping the rest of the Division. There we waited for the enemy to advance and although the barrage was very heavy and our casualties considerable the spirit was remarkable. I should have mentioned that a ground mist hung over everywhere until well after noon making it very difficult to see what was happening round about. After an incessant bombardment for 5 or 6 hours the barrage lifted when we started sniping and emptying Lewis gun magazines into Fritz who showed no anxiety to get to close quarters on account of what he had received from the Battalion in front of us and whom had been taken to another position leaving us the front line. About 4 p.m. we moved across to our positions as per arrangement which were in front, half right, but after spending a couple of hours there working like trojans improving the trenches we returned to our original flank position where we spent the night in clearing up our trenches and making preparations for the morrow.

(sd) GEO.M.KEVAN, Corporal,
10 Platoon 'Y' Company.
2/8/18.

9 Platoon 'Y' Company.

On the morning of 9th April 1918 our billets at MESPLAUX FARM were subjected to shell fire. At about 4.30 a.m. orders were given to proceed to our special positions which were allotted to us in case of an offensive by the Germans. We had barely started on our way when Jerry sent over a number of heavy shells which caused a number of casualties. Carrying on in good spirits we wended our way through the village of LE HAMEL and there we had a much livelier time of it as the bombardment increased and an enormous number of gas shells landed round about us. This necessitated putting on Box Respirators which consequently slackened our progress a good deal. After about 5 minutes we left the gas behind us. Carrying on we reached the village of LOISNE and once again we had to take the necessary precautions against gas. It was at this point we were directed into a trench which lay about 1500 yards in front of LOISNE CHATEAU. Our original position was about 500 yds in front and over to the right but owing to the retirement of the Portuguese nobody was manning this next trench, so acting on the instructions of Lieut. MONKHOUSE who was in charge of our platoon we decided to remain. At this time the bombardment was very severe and our trench was subjected to a heavy gas barrage which lasted about six hours. All this time a heavy mist was hanging around so consequently we could not see anything that was happening in front of us. The mist cleared at about 2 o'clock and then we found that we were actually in the front line with the enemy about 600 yards away, which we surmised was ROUTE A KEEP. We immediately opened fire and good results we obtained as a number of the enemy were seen to be wounded. Night rolled on and we worked hard and converted the trench into something like a fighting trench. From this night until the night of the 12th/13th inst. we occupied these trenches keeping a very keen look out and repairing trench. Then we took over CAILLOUX KEEP South just after the enemy had been driven out. For four days we held this position during which time barely a shell was fired on us. We were subsequently relieved on the night of the 16th/17th inst.

           (sd) S.E. COLLINS,
             Sergeant,
          No. 9 Platoon, 'Y' Company.
            2-8-1-8.

Notes on Operations 9/4/18 - 16/4/18
'X' Coy. 1/10th (Scottish) Bn. K.L.R.

On the morning of the 9/5/18 about 3.30 am. the Coy. who were then occupying rest billets in LE HAMEL were awakened by heavy enemy gun fire along the front - everyone immediately stood to and awaited orders. On orders received the Coy. proceeded by platoons to Bustle positions i.e., TUNING FORK LINE, a heavy mist hung over the ground and roads were heavily shelled by gas and H.E. shells, but we arrived in the allotted positions by app. 5.30 a.m.
'V' Coy. occupied positions on our right - 'Z' Coy. were on our left rear. A keen lookout was kept for enemy movement, whenever a target shewed L.G. and rifle fire was immediately opened. During the days of the 9th & 10th our positions were under continuous shell-fire. On the night of the 10th/11th the Coy. moved forward and established ORCHARD POST.

At 8 a.m. on the 11th a hurricane bombardment was opened on our positions but no infantry action followed. During bombardment we lost (killed) the officer in charge and one complete L.G. team. I was then left in charge of post until another officer arrived on the morning of the 12th. The days 11th and 12th with the exception of the bombardment passed uneventful. On the night 12th/13th, 12 mid. the Coy. attacked enemy post S.E. ROUTE A KEEP in conjunction with a Coy. of the 13th K.L.R. who were attacking ROUTE A KEEP. The attack was very successful five of the enemy being killed, 9 prisoners and 1 M.G. captured. We occupied the post until relieved by a Coy. of the 13th K.L.R. at 5 a.m. We then proceeded to the TUNING FORK LINE. 10 p.m. night 13th/14th we moved up to FESTUBERT and relieved a Coy. of the 13th K.L.R.. After 48 hours which passed uneventful we were relieved by the Glos. Regt. night of the 16th/17th.

(Signed) F.CRANE.
Sergt.

'X' Coy. 1/10th Liverpool Scottish.
Operations from April 9th - 16th.,

At 3.30 a.m. on the morning of the 9th April while on rest in billets at LE HAMEL the Coy. was awakened by a heavy bombardment along the whole front, numerous shells falling close to the billets. The Coy. immediately 'stood to'.

On the orders of the O.C., Coy. The Coy. moved off by platoons to the 'BUSTLE' position in the TUNING FORK LINE.

In spite of the heavy mist and the roads being heavily shelled the Coy. succeeded in reaching their allotted positions in the TUNING FORK EAST LINE by approximately 5.30 a.m.

During the days of the 9th and 10th April the Company were under continual shell fire and the casualties were fairly heavy. On the night of the 10th/11th the Coy. moved forward and established ORCHARD POST.

About 8 a.m. on the morning of the 11th the enemy opened a hurricane bombardment for about 20 minutes on our posts during which we had the misfortune to lose the Officer in charge and a Lewis gun team, command being taken by the senior sergeant.

The days of the 11th and 12th passed uneventfully.

At midnight on the 12th the Coy. made an attack on an enemy post S.E. of ROUTE A KEEP working in conjunction with 13th K.L.R. Our attack was very successful 5 of the enemy were killed, 9 taken prisoners, 1 machine gun captured. The post was taken over by the 13th K.L.R. on the morning of the 13th, 'X' Coy. returning to their old position in the TUNING FORK EAST LINE.

The same night the Coy. moved up to FESTUBERT to relieve the 13th Bn.K.L.R. in FESTUBERT E.KEEP and FESTUBERT SOUTH positions.

The following 48 hours passed uneventfully, only for heavy shelling by the enemy.

On the night of the 15th/16th the Coy. was relieved by a Coy. of the GLOUCESTER Regt.,

(sd) J.B.WILSON, Cpl.

Army Form C. 2118.

WAR DIARY
or
INTELLIGENCE SUMMARY.
(Erase heading not required.)

Instructions regarding War Diaries and Intelligence Summaries are contained in F. S. Regs., Part II. and the Staff Manual respectively. Title pages will be prepared in manuscript.

Place	Date	Hour	Summary of Events and Information	Remarks and references to Appendices
			Capt. A.P. DICKINSON of "Z" Coy. Army was formed from the two Battns. and including Capt. A.B.J. HOUGHTON and 2/Lt. T.W. PILKINGTON from this Battn. Preparations for the departure of this personnel and of the remainder of the 2/10 Battn., were set on foot.	
			Casualties for the month:-	
			Officers	
			Killed	
			Capt. H. MACKAY. M.C. 10/4/18 (4th Cameron Hdrs.)	
			2/Lt. T.J. PRICE (Died of wounds) 25/4/18	
			" H.F. CRIGHTON 10/4/18	
			" J.K. THURLOW 24/4/17 4	
			Missing	
			V. 2/Lt. J.E. MOFFAT 9/4/18 1	
			Wounded	
			2/Lt. G.N. ROME 13/4/18	
			" G.M. BAKER 9/4/18	
			Capt. L.R.A. GATEHOUSE 9/4/18	
			2/Lt. A. ARBUCKLE 11/4/18	
			" J.T. MONKHOUSE 9/4/18	
			" B. HOLIFORD 10/4/18	
			" R. CROOKS 9/4/18 7	
			Total 12	
			O. Ranks	
			Killed and Died of Wounds. 81	
			Wounded 177	
			Missing 5	
			263	

D.C.A. Munro
Major
Lieut. Col.
Comdg. 1/10 (Scottish) Bn. King's Liverpool Regt.

WAR DIARY
or
INTELLIGENCE SUMMARY.

Army Form C. 2118.

Place	Date	Hour	Summary of Events and Information	Remarks and references to Appendices
	26° April		Enemy attacked craters in GIVENCHY neighbourhood in the evening & re-took "ROUTE A" KEEP.	
			Throughout the day 27 April vicial artillery fire	
			heavy bombardment of the enemys Y, Z & V Coys "stood to" but	
			no infantry action took place at 3.20 pm, owing to a very	
			Battn was relieved during the night - the 2nd Battn by 16° KRR	
			and 1st Battn by 1/7 KLR - and proceeded to billets in LABOURSE	
	28° April		Tactical discussion under G.O.C at 5 pm for C.O.s, 2nds	
			O/C Coys and adjutants. Enemy artillery active during the	
			night on gun positions most in vicinity of LABOURSE 29° April	
			on a number of villages. Hostile shelling of LABOURSE Battn moved	
			to billets in VAUDRICOURT. A 30 April the official amalgamation	
			of the two Battns took place during the day 2/9 O'Rourke	
			were transferred from the 2nd Battn and temporarily posted	
			to the corresponding Coys of this Battn. The following	
			officers were taken on the strength of the Battn:-	
			Captains H.T.WHITSON, A.P.DICKINSON, P.CARNELLEY, Lieuts E.O.JEPSON	
			E.H.S.DUCKWORTH, 2nd Lieuts G.R.KEIG, S.STEAD, P.St.J.RATHBONE	
			H.J.WHITE, J.L.DALE, E.I.McOLYMONT, H.RIDEHALGH, A.GEMMELL	
			R.S.CROSS, H.HENDERSON, R.H.COOPER, W.R.DOUGLAS and G.R.C.MOY;	
			and Capt H.T.WHITSON assumed command of "V" Coy and	

WAR DIARY
or
INTELLIGENCE SUMMARY.
(Erase heading not required.)

Army Form C. 2118.

Place	Date	Hour	Summary of Events and Information	Remarks and references to Appendices

23 April. The 2/10 (SCOTTISH) BN K.L.R. joined Battn about 1.30am and were disposed of as follows:— "C" Coy in TUNING FORK SWITCH, "D" Coy at WINDY CORNER, "B" Coy in TUNING FORK N and S KEEP, and "A" Coy in reserve in front of "X" Coy. Wood was received that 2/5 Y G.N ROME had been awarded the military cross in recognition of his bravery on 3 April when he captured a prisoner. The enemy support lines intermittent shelling of GORRE during the morning.

24 April at 4 am "X" Coy and 1 platoon of 2 Coy carried out a very successful counter-attack on route "A" KEEP. The KEEP was captured with 11 prisoners, 1 heavy and 4 light machine guns. During G.O.C. and B.G.C. visited B" HQR in the afternoon.

The night "X" Coy in ROUTE "A" KEEP was relieved by B" Coy 2/10 K.L.R.

25 April. ROUTE "A" KEEP shells observed continuously throughout the day. Otherwise the situation was fairly quiet. "X" Coy moved to huts in vicinity of Burgade HQR about 8.30 pm.

Battn was relieved during the night by banks of 5/8 + 6/4 SOUTH STAFFS. RGT and 6 N STAFF RGT (137 Brigade 46 Div) and whole moved to positions as follows:— "C" and "A" Coys (2n Battn) relief of two coys 1/5 S.LANCS RGT from BARNTON ROAD to LE PLANTIN SOUTH (warehouse); "B" and "D" Coys (2n Battn) to WINDY CORNER SWITCH on left and night flank of "V" Coys; "Y" Coy to MARAIS, E. KEEP and posts in vicinity; Z Coy to LE PREOL LOCALITY.

Reliefs were completed by 5 am

WAR DIARY or INTELLIGENCE SUMMARY

Army Form C. 2118.

Place	Date	Hour	Summary of Events and Information	Remarks and references to Appendices
	April 15th		Enemy opened a very heavy bombardment at 9 a.m. on the whole FESTUBERT LOCALITY which was continued intermittently the whole day. Battn was relieved at night by 2 coys 12th GLOUCESTER REGT and 1 coy S. WALES. BORDER. R., and on relief proceeded to BEURY and thence by bus to RAIMBERT – arriving in billets at 4.0. a.m.	
	16th April		Reinforcements reports for duty, 3 officers arrived during the evening.	
	17th April		Bay spent in cleaning up, consent in the evening.	
	18th April		Parades under Coy arrangements.	
	19th April		G.O.C. inspected the Battn and delivered a short speech. He was heartily cheered by all ranks.	
	20th April		Parades under Coy arrangements. Bn entrained at about 4.30 pm and proceeded to VERQUIN – where billets were allotted.	
	21st April		Battn paraded at 12 noon and was addressed by the B.G.C. In the evening Battn paraded and proceeded to support trenches in relief of 1st GLOUCESTER REGT. – dispositions being as follows:– HQrs in GORRE CHATEAU. 'V' Coy in TUNING FORK SOUTH. 'X' Coy in trenches at S.E. corner of GORRE WOOD. 'Y' Coy in trenches at N and E corner of GORRE WOOD and 'Z' Coy on right of 'X' Coy, running from TUNING FORK ROAD to the CANAL. Relief was complete about 1 a.m. and a new trench was commenced behind stream 500 yards E. of GORRE WOOD.	
	22nd April		Enemy opened a heavy bombardment at 4 a.m. on LOISNE and ROUTE "A" KEEP – capturing the battn. place. During the day, orders were received that the 2/10th (SCOTTISH) BN. K. L. R. would join the Battn with a view to amalgamation.	

WAR DIARY or INTELLIGENCE SUMMARY

Army Form C. 2118.

The Battn was disposed as follows:- HQrs in FESTUBERT, "J" Coy in CAILLOUX S. KEEP and McMAHON TRENCH, "X" Coy in the TUNING FORK SWITCH LINE, "V" Coy in the TUNING FORK LINE and "Z" Coy in LOISNE CENTRAL.

12th April Visibility very good. FESTUBERT shelled throughout the day at midnight a counter-attack was made on ROUTE "A" KEEP by "X" Coy and "D" Coy 13th B.W.L.R. (under the command of His Battn's Commdg Officer). The enterprise was very successful — 9 prisoners being taken and a number of the enemy killed. "X" Coy's objective was the enemy trench and M.G. position immediately S. of the KEEP.

As a result of the fighting in the KEEP could be heard at 1.30 am. (the objective of "D" Coy 13 B.W. K.L.R.) Capt. J R McSWINEY (O.C. "X" Coy) personally carried out a reconnaissance and found that only 10 of the KEEP had been captured. Quickly returning a supply of bombs, he effectually drove the enemy from the remainder of the KEEP.

Later the enemy counter-attacked, but a counter-attack to regain possession, but was driven off with heavy loss.

In the early morning and of the enemy surrendered himself to the garrison of CAILLOUX KEEP. FESTUBERT was heavily shelled throughout the afternoon. **13th April** The following relief took place in the early morning — "X" Coy to FESTUBERT E and support and "V" Coy to FESTUBERT C.T. and Advanced Posts, "Y" Coy to CAILLOUX N & S — all in relief of 13th B.K.L.R. "Z" Coy moved up to ROUTE "A" KEEP and HQrs to McMAHON TR. Relief was complete by 5 am. FESTUBERT again received considerable attention from 8" shells being used with some frequency

WAR DIARY
INTELLIGENCE SUMMARY.
(Erase heading not required.)

Army Form C. 2118.

Place	Date	Hour	Summary of Events and Information	Remarks and references to Appendices
			The Battn received orders to relieve parts of the PORTUGUESE DIV. the following day. 9th April at 4 am a very heavy bombardment on both the front and back areas opened and about 4.45 am the pre-arranged code-word "BUSTLE" (on receipt of which battle positions has to be occupied) was received, and the Battn moved to TUNING FORK LOCALITY. Heavy casualties were encountered en route, owing to the heavy and accurate shelling of all roads and tracks with H.E. and gas shells. Shelling continued heavily until 9.30 am, when the enemy attacked on a long front. On the unsuspected front of the battle, the attack was unsuccessful but on the left, the front occupied by the PORTUGUESE was penetrated and it was necessary to form a defensive flank in this direction. "Z" Coy accordingly occupied LOISNE CENTRAL. The Battn came under the orders of the 164. 165 Infantry Brigade. The evening and night were comparatively quiet. 10th April "Z" Coy were attacked three times during the day, but with great loss to the enemy on each occasion with 10 heavy losses. In the last attack, 2 machine guns and prisoners were captured. During the day, enemy aeroplanes leaving British markings dropped bombs on GORRE. 11th April enemy heavily bombarded the TUNING FORK LINE between 7.15 am and 8.15 am. In the evening orders were received that HQs and 1 Coy of the Battn would move to FESTUBERT in relief of 5th Bn. K.L.R. This move was completed satisfactorily by 4 am	

WAR DIARY
or
INTELLIGENCE SUMMARY

Army Form C. 2118.

1/10 [Liverpool?] V.P.

April 1918

Place	Date	Hour	Summary of Events and Information	Remarks and references to Appendices
In the field	30.4.18		On April 1st Battn were occupying front line and support trenches in the section immediately South of the LA BASSEE CANAL. The enemy artillery were rather active, also his aeroplanes - which succeeded in bringing down five of our observation balloons. A lecture was given in the afternoon by G.O.C. 55 Division at Brigade HQs with on "The German offensive and how it affects the Division." 2nd April during the morning 900 shells used during the day. Orders were received that enemy were must fire (here named SS.S.A.A. doubly and this mention was consequently set for force. 3rd April 2nd Lt. G.N. ROME (Battn. scout officer) and 12 men carried out a very successful entrance - taking the enemy trenches in the early morning, killing 2 of the enemy and bringing back one prisoner, hardly obtaining valuable indentifications. 4th April The Battn snipers whilst watching round "BABY CRATER" were particularly successful. Two of the enemy in TWIN SAP. Two fast were killed by the snipers. The corps commandant visited the Battn during the day and expressed his satisfaction with the appearance of the men.. A patrol which was out opposite TWIN SAP was fired on by a M.G. and 12 bombs were thrown at them causing one casualty. 35 other Rank Reinforcements joined the Battn. April 5' and 6 spasmodic shelling. Congratulatory telegrams received from G.O.C. B.G.C. regarding 2nd Lt Rome's exploits and Lt Baron was relieved in the evening by 2/5th K.R.R. (1st Brigade 1st Div) and proceeded to billets in LE QUESNOY 2 Cos being battn HQs at BEUVRY. Still 2 (No 2 Co(s) (& Nos 2 mortars) to MESPLAUX FARM. Battn locates at BEUVRY. Two Cos and billets at LE HAMEL.	

166th Brigade.
55th Division.

1/10th BATTALION

THE KING'S LIVERPOOL REGIMENT

APRIL 1918.

WAR DIARY
or
INTELLIGENCE SUMMARY.
(Erase heading not required.)

Army Form C. 2118.

Date	Hour	Summary of Events and Information	Remarks and references to Appendices
MARCH 1918		**3-1-18 (cont)** Bn then moved to trenches in VILLAGE LINE and CAMBRIN LOCALITY, in relief of 1/6 N STAFFS REGT (137 Bde) **28-3-18** Battn relieved 2 coys 1/5 S Lancs and front of coys of 1/5 K.O.R.L. in right sector of new Brigade front. Dispositions were *Keen Jy* and "X" coys in front line, Z & J coys in support in VILLAGE LINE a new Bn HQrs were established behind VILLAGE LINE and arrangements were put in hand immediately for their improvement. Artillery on both sides very quiet. During night J coy moved up to centre position on Bn front. **29-3-18.** Z coy moved up into close support in the reserve line, and 1 coy 1/5 S Lancs Regt. was attached to Battn, and garrisoned VILLAGE LINE from LEWIS KEEP to BURBURE ALLEY. Enemy artillery inactive. **30-3-18** Wet weather. Quiet day. **31-3-18.** Easter Sunday. R. of E. chaplain celebrated communion in church dug-out. Except for shelling of back areas, enemy artillery quiet. Small parties sent to ANNEQUIN for bathing.	

Casualties.

	Officers	O Ranks
Killed in Action	—	4
Died of Wounds.	—	1
Wounded.	1.	11
	1.	16.

RCA Munro Major
~~Lieut Col~~
Commdg. 1/10 (Scottish) Bn. King's Liverpool Regt.

WAR DIARY or INTELLIGENCE SUMMARY

Army Form C. 2118.

Place	Date	Hour	Summary of Events and Information	Remarks and references to Appendices
	MARCH 1918.		20-3-18 (contd) Hon Capt A.C. JACK proceeded to England for tuition of duty, and Capt. H. MACKAY, M.C. temporarily took over duties of Q.M. The Battn. joining XI Corps was inspected by the new Corps Commander, Lt. Genl. Sir R.C.B. HAKING, K.C.B., K.C.M.G., inspected coys on any parade grounds, on conclusion of which he addressed the Offrs and N.C.O.s of Hon 2/5 and QM G.T.COULSON, 9th Bn D.L.I. joined Battn and took over duties of Q.M. <u>21-3-18</u> Normal offensive commenced on front of 3rd and 5th Armies training under any arrangements carried out, in mild weather. <u>22-3-18</u> Training under any arrangements at noon the B.& C declined to all officers and N.C.O's boys at LE HAMEL were visited by Bn Bomont Party, who gave them a most appreciated performance. <u>23-3-18</u> Training under any arrangements in the afternoon, while officers were engaged in Lecture exercises, a platoon b a side football competition was commenced all leave stopped and students and staff from schools commenced to return <u>24-3-18</u> Sunday Naval church parades held. Football competition won (after 2 replays) by transport against Y coy in the evening the Duol Bomont Party gave an enjoyable out-of-doors programme. <u>25-3-18</u> Stand to ordered at 4am until 8-30 am, after which usual training was carried on. Major W.M. PHILLIPS ordered to report his unit, and Major D.C.D MUNRO, M.C., D.C.M. assumed command at 10 p.m. Battn was ordered to move at midnight, and after divergent orders Battn eventually moved to TUNING FORK LOCALITY and were in allotted positions by 3 ad no unusual situation having arisen Battn moved back to billets animing Runt at 11-30 p.m. Reconnaissances were carried out, in the afternoon, of the CAMBRIN LOCALITY, in anticipation of possible move there in evening <u>26-3-18</u> Battn entrained for ANNEQUIN	

WAR DIARY
or
INTELLIGENCE SUMMARY.

(Erase heading not required.)

Army Form C. 2118.

Place	Date	Hour	Summary of Events and Information	Remarks and references to Appendices
	MARCH		19-3-18 (contd) None of the enemy wire encountered, and it appeared that the enemy was not manning his front line. Little retaliation was experienced in reply to our bombardment. The Battn was relieved without enemy interfering between 1 pm and 4 pm by 1/4th Bn K.L.R. and proceeded into Divl Reserve (Battn H.Q. & coy at MESPLAUX FARM, 2 coys at LE HAMEL). The Battn was under one hours notice (except between hours of 5 am and 9 am, when Battn was under ½ an hour notice) to turn out in event of code words "BUSTLE" or "PORT" being received, in accordance with orders issued. 18-3-18 Summer weather. Troops in readiness for either code words being received. The daily routine was changed, Reveillé to 4 am and "Lights out" was played at 8 p.m. after Coy Commanders' conference. Careful reconnaissance was carried out by all officers and senior N.C.O.s, of battle positions in event of code word "PORT" full use was made of Baths allotted. 19-3-18 Warning orders were amended to read Battn at 1 hours notice all day; in consequence of which movement routine hours were respected to 1.a.p. were engaged in cleaning up and bathing. Major D.C.D MUNRO, M.C, D.C.M, 1st (Gordon H'landrs) arrived from England and assumed duties of Second in command. 10% of each coy was allowed on pass to BETHUNE, and during the evening this town was heavily shelled and bombed. 20-3-18 The commanding officer inspected the Battn in the morning at MESPLAUX a motor 'bus was placed at the disposal of Battn for purpose of conveying a limited number who were desirous of visiting the 2nd BN at ESTAIRES. A successful concert was given by a Battn concert party at MESPLAUX.	

WAR DIARY
or
INTELLIGENCE SUMMARY.
(Erase heading not required.)

Army Form C. 2118.

Place	Date	Hour	Summary of Events and Information	Remarks and references to Appendices
	12-3-18 (contd)		"V" coy rejoined Battn. Major T.A. RODDICK, M.C. proceeded to Corps Rest Station, and Major W.M. PHILLIPS, 1/5th K.O.R.L. Regt took over temporary command.	
	13-3-18		Exceptionally quiet day. Patrols had nothing unusual to report.	
	14-3-18		Weather changed - cold, mist and rain. Patrols returned at 5-15 hrs and our sector was subjected to a heavy bombardment at 5-15 hrs and our artillery retaliated effectively. The artillery duel died down about 1-30 p.m. Our casualties - 2 men killed. Patrols reconnoitred the condition of wire in front of enemy trenches, which a coy of 1/5th K.O.R.L. Regt. proposed to raid at a later date. Patrols reported artillery had effectually cut gaps in enemy wire, but that in scout officer's opinion, the enemy front line was not manned. At 6 p.m. the enemy artillery code-word "BUSTLE" was received and Battn. "stood to". Enemy artillery fired spasmodically during the evening. Major T.A. RODDICK, M.C. proceeded on leave to England from Corps Rest Station.	
	15-3-18		Battn. stood down at 8 am. Enemy artillery very aggressive, and 4 casualties were sustained (1 killed, 2 died of wounds, 1 wounded). Constant patrolling was carried out, and our Lewis Gunners gave enemy no opportunity of repairing the gaps in this wire.	
	16-3-18		Weather fine. FESTUBERT shelled from 9am to 9.30 am. Orders were received for reconnaissance to be carried out of positions that would be taken up by Battn. when in Divisional Reserve on receipt of codeword "PORT" (this codeword being intimation to move up in support of Portuguese Division on our left). Same was carried out. Patrols reported gaps in wire still satisfactory.	
	17-3-18		Proceeded by heavy bombardment, a coy of the 1/5th KORL raided enemy trenches	

WAR DIARY
or
INTELLIGENCE SUMMARY.
(Erase heading not required.)

Army Form C. 2118.

MARCH 1918

Place	Date	Hour	Summary of Events and Information	Remarks and references to Appendices
MARCH 1918	1-3-18		The Battn in trenches, GIVENCHY SECTION. Quiet day. Patrols sent out at night reported no unusual movement.	
	2/3/18.		Work was concentrated upon wiring of PRINCES ISLAND, and for this purpose every available man utilised	
	4-3-18		The Battn (less 1 coy) was relieved by 1/7th Bn K.L.R. and became support Battn (1 coy & Bn HQrs at GORRE, and remaining 2 coys at FERME DU ROI) "X" coy were left behind as wiring party for PRINCES ISLAND. The dispositions of the Division were re-organised, and the sector for each Brigade was considerably shortened.	
	5-3-18		"X" coy relieved by coy of 1/5 S.Lancs and joined Battn in support at GORRE. Whilst on wiring 2&Lt. E McCALLUM and 1 O/Rank were wounded. About this time, daily information was received that prisoners recently captured on Corps front reported an attack imminent on our sector. Sound observers reported unusual movement and activity. All Battns were warned to be ready on alert, and code-word "BUSTLE" was initiated, and, on receipt of this code-word, units were to move to pre-arranged battle positions, in accordance with Defence Scheme.	
	6-3-18.		Battn supplied working and carrying parties in afternoon and evening.	
	7-3-18	5-20 am	Battn "stood-to", and moved to pre-allotted battle positions in TUNING FORK LOCALITY. On situation becoming quiet the Battn returned to billets. GORRE was lightly shelled during day, and Battn had one man slightly wounded.	
	8-3-18		"V" coy relieved 1 coy of 1/5th King's own in front line, and came under orders of O.C. 1/5 K.O.R.L. Regt. 9-3-18—11-3-18 Weather continued fine. Battn engaged on working parties.	
	12-3-18		Battn (less V coy) relieved 1/5th KORL in daylight in front line	

9/11/39

War Diary
of
1/10th Liverpool R
1st tenure
1st to 31st March
1918

WAR DIARY or INTELLIGENCE SUMMARY

Army Form C. 2118.

Place	Date	Hour	Summary of Events and Information	Remarks and references to Appendices
	19th – 24th Feb.		Parades under Coy arrangements – special attention being paid to gas precautions. Working parties were supplied daily. Commdg Officer lectured to Officers and N.C.O's each afternoon. Reconnaissance of both forward and back areas by Officers and N.C.O's. On 21st Feb, the Commdg Officer, Adjt, and O.C. Coys attended a tactical exercise under the Major General Commdg. On 23rd Feb the same Officers attended a tactical scheme by the Major General Commdg.	
	25th Feb		The Battn rejoined 166 Inf. Brigade and relieved 1/5 K.L.R. in night subsection, left section (NORTH of LA BASSÉE CANAL) – three Coys being in the front line and one in support. Relief was reported complete at 1.0 pm.	
	26th Feb		1/5 O/Ranks Reinforcements. Little enemy artillery activity. 27th Feb. Enemy reported our trenches in the evening causing one casualty.	
	28th Feb		Patrols were sent out each night. The Battn were in the trenches – bringing back information as to enemy work at Makens again quiet.	

Total casualties for month :- 1 O/Rank wounded

Jas Arthur?
Commdg. 1/10 (Scottish) Bn. King's Liverpool Regt.

WAR DIARY
INTELLIGENCE SUMMARY
(Erase heading not required.)

Army Form C. 2118.

Place	Date	Hour	Summary of Events and Information	Remarks and references to Appendices
	1/2/18		Battn. in billets in BEAUMETZ-LEZ-AIRES. Kit inspections and practice "stand-to" carried out followed by inspection by the Commdg. Officer. 2nd Febr. Battn. moves to LAIRES to witness Brigade Inter platoon A.R.A. competition. "X" Coy gaining 2nd place in the competition. 3rd Feb. Sunday. 4th Feb. Individual & platoon training. Tactical exercise for all officers. 5th Feb. Individual & platoon training — firing at disappearing targets. Demonstration of rapid fire. Installation holding holiday at services of the award of the Belgium "CROIX DE GUERRE" to 4/C. R. DUTTON. 6th Feb. Holiday. 7th Feb. Owing to bad weather day was spent in lectures on ammunition economy. 8th Feb. inspections and preparations made for the move the following day. 9th Feb. Battn. paraded at 9.0 a.m. and marched to WESTREHEM — a distance of about six miles. 10th Feb. Continuation of move. Battn. of 14 miles to LARGNOY — arriving in billets by 4.0. p.m. 11th Feb. Day spent in cleaning up – inspections by O/s. C. Coys. 12th Feb. Battn. came under orders of Brigadier Genl. Commdg. 56 164th Inf Brigade and moved to VERQUIN by march route. 13th Feb. Officers recconoitred the village defences and back areas. 14th Feb. Battalion moves to LE PREOL into Brigade Reserve. 15th Feb. Parades under Coy arrangements. Junior recconoisance of defences by Officers & N.C.O's. Officers in 3 O/Ranks reinforcements joined Battn. "Stand-to" practices in the evening. 16th Feb. Boy parades. Lecture to all officers by Commdg. Officer. "Stand-to's" 17th Feb Sunday. Church parades and practise "Stand to". Lt. Col. T. A. MACDONALD. D.S.O. Major T. A. RODDICK. M.C. proceeds on one months leave to England. 18th Feb. assumes command of the Battn.	

War Diary
of the
1/10th Liverpool R.
for the period

1st to 28th Feby
1918

WAR DIARY / INTELLIGENCE SUMMARY

Army Form C. 2113.

Place	Date	Hour	Summary of Events and Information	Remarks and references to Appendices
	18/1/18		Battn Route march (tactical) followed by Inter-Coy & Personnel wiring Party. Both competitions were won by 1500 Battn & by "X" Coy & of Pte Bowd Transport competition was held in the afternoon which was attended by the Major-General Commanding & Brigadier General.	
	20/1/18		Church Parade. Platoon wiring inter-platoon & football competitions. Lecture to N.C.O's by Adjutant.	
	21/1/18		No Parades. Holiday granted to Battn by Brig-General Commdg.	
	22/1/18		Platoon Training all-day.	
	23/1/18		Platoon Training all-day. Platoons engaged in packing for R.A. competition by Brig-General.	
	24/1/18		4 Officers & 67 O/Ranks Reinforcements reported for duty.	
	25/1/18		Training under Coy arrangements.	
	26/1/18		Church Parade.	
	27/1/18		R.A. Competition held — won by "X" Coy. Night operations.	
	28/1/18		Brigade Training at ERNY - ST JULIEN. Brigadier General witnessed same.	
	29/1/18		Presented to all Ranks in the Brigade Medals to same. Re inturned of the "1914" Star. 1 Officer Reinforcement reports for duty.	
	30/1/18		Holiday given by Brigadier General. Battn witnessed Divisional wiring competition, which "X" Coy obtained across prize.	
	31/1/18		Route march.	
			Casualties for week :- NIL	

Commdg. 1/10 (Scottish) Bn. King's Liverpool Regt.

WAR DIARY or INTELLIGENCE SUMMARY

Army Form C. 2118.

H.Q. 186TH INFANTRY BDE.

Place	Date	Hour	Summary of Events and Information	Remarks and references to Appendices
In the field	1/1/18		Battn in billets in village of BEAUMETZ-LEZ-AIRE. Mobility competitions were carried out.	
	2/1/18		Training in outpost duties and continuation of musketry competitions.	
	3/1/18		Training - charge and march past, followed by mobility competitions of Platoon & Company Training. 4/1/18 Brigade Platoons in the "advance" in matters inspected by the Brig. General commanding "The Platoon in the advance" in which bombing was awarded the B.S.O.	
	5/1/18		News that Lt. Col. J.L.A. MACDONALD (Commdg) has been awarded the D.S.O.	
	6/1/18		Battn parades for Divine Service. 7/1/18 Training by Coys in musing musketry, bombing & bayonet fighting.	
	8/1/18		Day Training. All Officers & N.C.O's paraded for "Rabi's" winning Tactical scheme for Officers, under the commanding officer.	
	9/1/18		Owing to severe weather outside parades were impracticable. Lectures being given in the billets. Notification received on 30/1/17:- 2nd Bar to Military Medal - 11. 11/1/18 Brigade Rapid Firing competition. The following demonstrations for gallantry and devotion to duty. Training under Sn Capt arrangements. Rabis winning competition for N.C.O's: Tactical scheme for Officers. 1 Officer and 5 or Ranks attended demonstration of rapid loading and Lewis gun and firing under Brig. Genl Commdg. 12/1/18 Brigade demonstrations and rebates for duty. 13/1/18 Church parade. 14/1/18 Brigade demonstration. Musketry competitions. 15/1/18-16/1/18 Lectures. The Brigade-Major gave lecture on musketry.	
	17/1/18		Demonstration of semi-open warfare by a selects platoon. Training again intended, owing to weather. 18/1/18 Training again intended with by making minimet weather.	

Ys 37

War Diary
of the
1/10th Liverpool R
for the period
1st to 31st January
1918.

Army Form C. 2118.

WAR DIARY
or
INTELLIGENCE SUMMARY.
(Erase heading not required.)

Instructions regarding War Diaries and Intelligence Summaries are contained in F.S. Regs., Part II. and the Staff Manual respectively. Title pages will be prepared in manuscript.

Place	Date	Hour	Summary of Events and Information	Remarks and references to Appendices
			On this day, about 3" snow fell & with the weather continued cold with occasional snow showers till the end of the month. Casualties 1 O/R wounded. J Wainwright Lt Col Commdg 1/5(C of L) Bn K.R.R.C	

WAR DIARY or INTELLIGENCE SUMMARY

Route to IZEL LES HAMEAUX, the move was continued on the 11th Dec. to BAILLEUL LES CORNAILLES, when the 73rd stays the night, continuing on arrival on the 3rd Dec. on the move up to

TRANGRYSCRÊ PY & BEAUMETZ LES AIRES. Canning & I travel took the Batten (?) — the move was well managed, being sorty shortly until the completion of the journey. 5th Bon & then too little accomodation. Billets were found, after that the Big General Sanderson in visit of the Bon. & ensuring for resting & enabling during its first week of the village for recreation, in visit of the Brannents.

The opening of the Brannent was observed, and a football field was supposed to be and a Batten Canteen opened, from the 16th of the end of the month & the move of the Batten line began the lotting. Recognizing the Batten guidance as found a space here to Lt J Platoon was the Brig General in the Batten. demonstration — Xmas Day — Christmas was the 18th inst.

Christmas was celebrated by dinners being given to the four Companies which were attended by their Officers, the Commanding Officer called to eat Christmas the Brigadier General visited the Battalion

WAR DIARY

INTELLIGENCE SUMMARY

Month of December 1917.

Army Form C. 2118.

(Erase heading not required.)

Instructions regarding War Diaries and Intelligence Summaries are contained in F. S. Regs., Part II. and the Staff Manual respectively. Title pages will be prepared in manuscript.

Place	Date	Hour	Summary of Events and Information	Remarks and references to Appendices
30 Nov	1 Dec 1917		At midnight the Battalion continued to put details to previous night. About 5.30 a.m. Capt. J.A. Roddick M.C. successful withdraw his garrison from LIMERICK Post and commenced digging in the valley South of FALLEN-TREE Post. No further attack by the enemy developed during the day. About 9.0 a.m. 2 Squadrons of Indian Cavalry attacked the enemy up FALLEN-TREE Road and the Valley on its South side, on arrival at KILDARE & LIMERICK Posts they were held up by heavy machine gun fire, & forced to withdraw. During the afternoon Brigadier General F.G. LEWIS C.B. commanding 166 Inf Bde was wounded and Lt Col J.A. MACDONALD assumed command of the Brigade, and Capt. J.A. RODDICK took command of the Battalion. On Dec. 2nd at 4 a.m. the Battn was relieved by the 9th Leicestershire Regt & marched to Billets in TINCOURT. Two Officers & 40 O/R Reinforcements arrived from the Divn Reinf. Depot Battn on Dec. 3rd. On Dec. 4th Brig. Gen. R. J. KENTISH D.S.O. arrived from England & took command of the 166 Inf Bde & Lt Col J.A. MACDONALD resumed command of the Battn. On Dec 5th the Battn commenced to move from TINCOURT to BEAUMETZ LES AIRES for reorganization & training. 1st Coys Over at BEAUMETZ LES AIRES for reorganization & training. The B.S. Marching to FLAMICOURT where the Battalion rested until the 8th when the move was continued by Train to AUBIGNY, arrived	

(A7991). Wt. W12839/M1293. 750,000. 1/17. D. D. & L., Ltd. Forms/C.2118/14.

War Diary
of the
1/10th Liverpool R.
for the period
1st to 31st December 1917.

Army Form C. 2118.

WAR DIARY
INTELLIGENCE SUMMARY.
(Erase heading not required.)

Nov 1917 (cont'd)

Place	Date	Hour	Summary of Events and Information	Remarks and references to Appendices
	Nov 30th cont'd		T.A. RODDICK, M.C., and his garrison were still in possession of the post. Casualties for month |	Officers	o/Ranks	Totals
---	---	---	---
Killed	-	8	8
Died of wounds	-	3	3
Missing	9	435	444
Wounded	1	66	67 | 522	

Munsterwal
Lt Col Commanding
1/10 (Scottish) Bn K.L.R.

Army Form C. 2118.

Nov. 1917 (contd)

WAR DIARY
INTELLIGENCE SUMMARY.
(Erase heading not required.)

Instructions regarding War Diaries and Intelligence Summaries are contained in F. S. Regs., Part II. and the Staff Manual respectively. Title pages will be prepared in manuscript.

Place	Date	Hour	Summary of Events and Information	Remarks and references to Appendices
	Nov: 30th (contd)		owing to large bodies of the enemy advancing down valleys from PIGEON QUARRY and threatening to outflank this position. Immediately it was 10.40 am the garrison retired fighting to the green line. Then the living established at S.E. corner of LIMERICK POST. KILDARE POST was occupied by remnants of the Battn. The enemy had penetrated a considerable distance to the rear and the position occupied by this Bn. was practically surrounded. Late in the afternoon it was considered advisable to withdraw garrison from KILDARE POST as all ammunition had been expended and no supplies or reinforcements were forthcoming. The withdrawal was successfully accomplished and posts established about 800 yards in rear from FALLEN TREE ROAD to the COPSE on the SOUTH. The garrison of LIMERICK POST were completely surrounded by 2/3 pm and no communication could be made with them. Several strong enemy attacks were made against this post during the afternoon and evening. It was later ascertained that all these attacks were beaten off with heavy losses to the enemy. At 12 midnight Capt.	

WAR DIARY
INTELLIGENCE SUMMARY.
(Erase heading not required.)

Army Form C. 2118.

Nov. cont[d]

Place	Date	Hour	Summary of Events and Information	Remarks and references to Appendices
		Nov. (cont[d])	penetrated quickly. 2 platoons in KILDARE POST counter attacked - one reinforcing the front line and the other garrisoning DADOS LOOP. A stand was made on SPRINT ROAD by details of Right Bn Holgro and one platoon from SUPPORTS but being outflanked on both sides from the direction of COX'S BK on the left and HOLTS BK on the right withdrew fighting and established themselves on the ridge running south from Bn Holgro (THE ADELPHI) The progress of events on the Left Front Coy area is unknown - as nobody returned after the initiation of the attack. The enemy barrage was exceptionally heavy on PIGEON QUARRY and the enemy attacked in great strength from the high ground to the north - taking it in the rear. Nothing further is known of subsequent events. The details of Bn Holgro at THE ADELPHI immediately the attack commenced deployed in the open on high ground about 60 yards E. of THE ADELPHI and opened rapid fire against PIGEON QUARRY and. This was continued until the position became untenable	

1/10th (SCOTTISH) BN. K.L.R.

WAR DIARY
of
INTELLIGENCE SUMMARY.
(Erase heading not required.)

Army Form C. 2118.

Month of NOVEMBER 1917

Place	Date	Hour	Summary of Events and Information	Remarks and references to Appendices
In the field			Nov. 1st. Battn occupying trenches near EPEHY Intr-coy reliefs were carried out at intervals of 3 days. On Nov. 10th two parties of 1 NCO and 19 each were detailed for attachment to 165 inf. Brigade. On Nov 20th in conjunction with an attack on either flank rapid fire was opened along the Battn frontage at "zero" hour. The enemy retaliation was slight and one casualty was sustained. For the succeeding few days official patrols were sent out both by day and night with the object of ascertaining if the enemy were showing signs of evacuation. The enemy were very much on the alert but no signs of withdrawal were noticeable. Enemy artillery was more active than usual on 28th and 29th Nov: - apparently registering on various parts of the Battn area. Our artillery carried out concentration shoots at intervals, M.G's co-operating. On the morning of the 30th Nov: at 7am the enemy opened heavy artillery fire against all trenches and occupied areas in the Battn sector and at about 8 am attacked in strong force. The Right Front Coy held up the direct attack, except on the extreme right, where the enemy	

156/55 WM 36

35 L

War Diary
of the
110th Constantinople R
for the Period
1st to 30th November
1917

Army Form C. 2118.

WAR DIARY
or
INTELLIGENCE SUMMARY.
(Erase heading not required.)

Place	Date	Hour	Summary of Events and Information	Remarks and references to Appendices
Inkerfield	31/10/17		Battn occupied the same positions on Oct 31st	
			Casualties for month :—	
			<table><tr><td></td><td>Officers</td><td>O. Ranks</td></tr><tr><td>Missing</td><td></td><td>1</td></tr><tr><td>Wounded</td><td>1</td><td>5</td></tr></table> (3 accidental)	
			[signed] Major LIEUT. COLONEL COMMANDING, 1/10th (SCOTTISH) Bn. KINGS (LIVERPOOL REGT.)	

WAR DIARY
or
INTELLIGENCE SUMMARY

Army Form C. 2118.

Place	Date	Hour	Summary of Events and Information	Remarks and references to Appendices
In the field	31/10/17		Platoon, Company and Battalion training, firing on range and the usual training was carried out daily whilst Battn. was at VILLERS-FAUCON. On Oct. 19th, the Battn. were inspected (as part of the Brigade) at LONGAVESNES by the General Officer Comm'dg. 55th Division. The following day, a Brigade tactical exercise in semi-open warfare was practised in the presence of Major-General WRIGHT, U.S.A. Army. The Battn. proceeded to trenches on Oct. 25th and relieved 1/4 K.L.R. in the same sector as previously occupied - relief being completed without incident by 9 p.m. The enemy artillery was active during the succeeding three days, shelling intermittently the front and support lines. Work was carried on as usual with satisfactory results - good progress being made. On 28th October inter-company relief took place, "Y" & "V" Coys. relieving "Z" & "X" Coys in the left and right sectors respectively. Owing to change in Brigade dispositions, 2 platoons moved from HOLTS BANK to KILDARE POST. Enemy artillery was again active on 29th Oct.	

WAR DIARY
INTELLIGENCE SUMMARY

October 1917

Place	Date	Hour	Summary of Events and Information	Remarks and references to Appendices
In the field	31/10/17		On 1st October Battn. was in trenches near EPEHY. Hands work was necessary on the trenches, and large parties were employed both by day and night improving parapets, deepening and widening trenches etc. The enemy artillery was generally inactive except for occasional bursts of shrapnel and a few 77 mm's. On Oct 6th an inter-Coy. relief was carried out "V" Coy relieving "X" Coy and "Z" Coy relieving "Y" Coy in the right and left subsectors respectively. Patrols, both reconnoitring and offensive were sent out each night and information as to the enemy's wire and defences obtained. Major J.L.A. MACDONALD proceeded to 3rd Army School for course on Oct. 8th and Capt. J A RODDICK. M.C., assumed command of the Battn. On Oct. 13th Battn was relieved by 119 K.L.R, and on relief marched to billets at VILLERS-FAUCON. Major J L A MACDONALD rejoined and assumed command of the Battn.	

WM 34

War Diary
of the
1/10th Liverpool R.
for the period
1st to 31st October 1917.

Army Form C. 2118.

WAR DIARY
or
INTELLIGENCE SUMMARY.
(Erase heading not required.)

Instructions regarding War Diaries and Intelligence
Summaries are contained in F. S. Regs., Part II.
and the Staff Manual respectively. Title pages
will be prepared in manuscript.

Place	Date	Hour	Summary of Events and Information	Remarks and references to Appendices
			On the 23rd Sept, Battn (two Coys) proceeded by motor lorry from VLAMERTINGHE to WATOU No 2 Area. The remaining two Coys, who had been attached to 164th Infantry Brigade, rejoined the Battn the following day. Battn entrained at PROVEN, on the 26th Sept, for MIRAUMONT, arriving at this latter place at 2 a.m. 27th Sept, and marched from thence to BEULENCOURT. On 29th Battn proceeded by road route to VILLERS-FAUCON, and on the following day marched to EPEHU, relieving 15th Battn CHESHIRE REGT. The relief was carried out without casualties by 10.30 p.m.	

Casualties for the month.

	Officers	O/Ranks	Total.
Wounded	1	50	51
Killed		13	13
Died of Wounds		2	2
			66

Manwaring
LIEUT-COLONEL
COMMANDING, 1/10th (SCOTTISH) BN. THE KINGS (LIVERPOOL R)

Army Form C. 2118.

WAR DIARY
or
INTELLIGENCE SUMMARY.
(Erase heading not required.)

Place	Date	Hour	Summary of Events and Information	Remarks and references to Appendices
			(3)	

attachment to 164th Infantry Brigade, and at 2 p m took up positions in the old German front line.

The remainder of the Battn were placed under the orders of the Brig-General Commdg. 165th Infantry Brigade. Consequently at 9.40 p.m the Battn (less two Coys) moved into a line of shell-holes in the vicinity of ELMS CORNER, in rear of HILL 37.

The enemy put up a heavy barrage the following morning principally at the foot of HILL 37. In the morning consequent upon the S.O.S being sent up from the immediate front two Coys, under command of MAJOR. J L A MCDONALD moved forward to reinforce the front line. As the situation, however, was well in hand on their arrival, one platoon took up a position near the CAPITOL, and a party of 1 Officer & 40 O/Ranks with two Lewis Guns reinforced the front line; the remainder re-occupying the position near ELMS CORNER.

The day of the 22nd Sept. passed uneventfully and Battn (less two Coys) were relieved in the evening by 2/6th NORTH. STAFFS. REGT, and proceeded on relief to bivouacs near GOLDFISH CHATEAU.

WAR DIARY
or
INTELLIGENCE SUMMARY.

(Erase heading not required.)

Army Form C. 2118.

Place	Date	Hour	Summary of Events and Information	Remarks and references to Appendices
			(2)	

On the night 15th Sept "V" Coy sent out a strong patrol to reconnoitre the enemy posts on the HANNEBEKE, with the object of capturing same, but were unable to secure the position. The following night a fighting patrol attempted to secure his position, but were unsuccessful.

On the night 14th Sept. Battn HQrs moved forward from CALL RESERVE to CAPRICORN KEEP and the two supporting Companies were relieved and proceeded to L4 Post near YPRES.

The same night two prisoners were taken by a forward post — having been driven towards our lines by our artillery barrage. "V" Coy also secured the required German positions on the HANNEBEEK.

The following evening, remaining two Coys. and Battn HQrs were relieved and proceeded to bivouacs at L4.

On the night of the 19th, Battn moved up to assembly positions in LIVERPOOL and S. BIRR TRENCHES and CONGREVE WALK, being in Divisional Reserve for the attack on the following day. Zero hour was at 5.40 a.m. and at 11.30 a.m. orders were received that Battn. would hold itself in readiness to move at 15 minutes notice. Two companies were detailed for

September 1917 WAR DIARY or INTELLIGENCE SUMMARY.

Army Form C. 2118.

Place	Date	Hour	Summary of Events and Information	Remarks and references to Appendices
In the field	31/9/16		Sept 1st. - Battn at ZOUAFQUES. - Brigade service carried out the following day, Sunday, a Brigade church service was held, followed by the presentation of ribands by Brigadier-General Commdg, to all who had been awarded decorations for gallantry in the recent operations. In the afternoon a Brigade Rifle meeting was held. The usual daily training was proceeded with until the 8th inst. On this date, Lt Col. T. R. DAVIDSON proceeded on leave to England, Major J. L. A. MACDONALD assuming command of the Battn. On Sept 10th part of Battn took train in 164B & 165B Brigade's service and acted as skeleton enemy. The following day word was received that Battn would move to forward area on 13th. These orders were subsequently confirmed and Battn paraded at 6.15 a.m. on this date, and proceeded by march route to AUDRUICQ, thence by train to GOLDFISH CHATEAU near YPRES. On Sept. 14th Battn marched to the trenches and relieved 2/5th GLOUCESTER. REGT. After relief, dispositions were as follows - Two Coys in FRONT LINE and two coys + Battn H.Q. in support line (2 PLT. RESERVE). The front line consisted of German concrete dugouts and gunpits, with a line of posts established, made by connecting shell-holes.	

166/55

Vol 33

332

CONFIDENTIAL

WAR DIARY

OF

1/10th LANCASHIRE R

FOR PERIOD

1/4/17 - 30/4/17

Army Form C. 2118.

WAR DIARY
—or—
INTELLIGENCE=SUMMARY.
(Erase heading not required.)

(Sheet III)
Summary of Events and Information

Place	Date	Hour		Remarks and references to Appendices
In the field	31/8/17		On 8th Aug. the Major-Gen. Comdg 55th Division inspected the Brigade and congratulated all ranks on their splendid work during the attack on July 31st. A draft of 62 O/Ranks reported for duty and a further draft of 267 O/Ranks on Aug 10th. From 9th Aug to 31st Aug training was carried out daily, special attention being paid to route marches, musketry and semi-open warfare, including field firing. On 13th Aug, 7 Officers Reinforcements joined the Battn. The following decorations were awarded for gallantry in the recent operations. Military Cross - Capt. J. A. RODDICK, Lieut W. E. PHILPOTTS, 2nd Lieut B. P. GALLOP and 2nd Lieut H. MACKAY, also C.S.M. B.A.B. MARPLES. D.C.M. - Two Bar to Military Medal - one. Military Medal - seventeen. On Aug 30th a Brigade exercise was carried out	

	OFFICERS.	O/RANKS
KILLED IN ACTION & DIED OF WOUNDS	4	51
WOUNDED	8	172
MISSING	-	6
Total casualties for month of August (including 31st July)	12	229

[signature] LIEUT.-COLONEL,
COMMANDING 1/10th (SCOTTISH) Bn. THE KINGS (LIVERPOOL REGT.)

WAR DIARY
INTELLIGENCE SUMMARY.
(Erase heading not required.)

(Sheet II)
Summary of Events and Information

Army Form C. 2118.

Place	Date	Hour	Summary of Events and Information	Remarks and references to Appendices
Wikefeld	31/8/17		They were unsuccessful, but later in the day were forced to retire to the BLACK LINE, owing to very heavy casualties and enemy fire. During the day, on several occasions, the enemy attempted to man for counter attack, but each time was dispersed by our artillery fire. Heavy rain set in and continued throughout the night. The subsequent two days were spent in holding the captured trenches which were in bad condition, owing to the severe weather. Enemy artillery fire during this period was very heavy, especially in the evenings and throughout the night. Battn was relieved in the early morning of the 3rd August by 11th Battn. INNISKILLING FUSILIERS and returned to LIVERPOOL & BILGE TRENCHES - the same night proceeding (by train from YPRES) to bivouacs near VLAMERTINGHE. Draft of 150 O/Ranks joined Battn. here. The following morning Battn. entrained at VLAMERTINGHE and proceeded to POPERINGHE; thence by march route to LEE and ESK camps near WATOU. On Aug. 6th Battn. entrained at ABEELE for AUDRUICQ, arriving at this latter place at about 6 am on 7th Aug, and marching from hence to billets at ZOUAFQUES.	

August 1917

WAR DIARY

INTELLIGENCE SUMMARY.

(Erase heading not required.)

Army Form C. 2118.

Place	Date	Hour	Summary of Events and Information	Remarks and references to Appendices
In the field	31/8/17		On July 31st, Battn took part in an attack on the enemy positions EAST of WIELTJE, in conjunction with Brigades R. on either flank. At 3.50 hours (3.50 a.m.) the 1/5. LOYAL N. LANCS REGT, under cover of artillery and machine gun barrage, advanced and easily seemed their objective – the BLUE LINE. This Battn, in 4 Companies, moved from assembly trenches in small columns, to the BLUE LINE, and whilst waiting for the barrage to lift, re-organised. Keeping close to the barrage, Companies advanced steadily and met with little opposition, until the STEENBEEK had been crossed, when heavy machine gun and rifle fire was encountered. The Battalion's objective, i.e. the BLACK LINE was ultimately secured with the aid of the Tanks, which put out of action the machine guns (firing from CAPRICORN TR.) which had held up the advance. The work of consolidation was proceeded with, the enemy's snipers meanwhile being very active and causing many casualties. At 10 a.m. the 164th Infy Brigade passed through our positions with the object of capturing the GREEN LINE.	

War Diary
of
1/10th Liverpool R
for period
1st to 31st August, 1917.

On the night of the 29th July 25 Officers & 445 O/R marches up for the attack, one Company occupying each of the following positions Congreve Walk, Liverpool Street, Kaie Salient, & Dixmude Street, no casualties were sustained whilst moving in.

As full particulars of the attack of the 31st are not yet to hand, the Battn being still in the line, casualties for the month are only calculated to the 30th July:-

Killed in Action   Officers – 4   O/R 12

Wounded   "   4   O/R 129.

M Davidson
Commanding 1/10 (Scot) Bn Kings Liverpool Rt

WAR DIARY
INTELLIGENCE SUMMARY.
(Erase heading not required.)

Army Form C. 2118.

Place	Date	Hour	Summary of Events and Information	Remarks and references to Appendices
			on July 30th	

all Bath arrived at 8:45 p.m. and moved to ST. OMER and remained at Wisques all around POPERINGHE at 12.30 p.m. after rest up at the base Camps. The Battn. proceeded by platoons to relieve various units & HAMPSHIRE section and relieved of 1st Lincs KRR. an enemy shell caused a considerable number of casualties, by the Canal Bank 2 killed and 1 officer & 7 O/R wounded.

On the night of the 21/22 the enemy who had made little reply to our active artillery put over a large amount of tear shells (Mustard Oil type), and in spite of all precautions being taken with Box Respirators, 2 Officers & 71 O/R were evacuated to Field Ambulance for gassing. Our own rifle & M.G. fire was kept up on the 3 following nights and efforts at various times after dawn, the enemy's gallows tree was never imminent.

Enemy artillery active against Alice Road Street on the morning 9th 24th the latter being damaged considerably.

At night of the same day the Battn. was relieved by 1st NORTHANTS & 1st Kings Liverpool and proceeded to DERBY Camp. near poperinghe. Our Casualties amounted to the 27th Oct. the Battn. should be approx. known at 30 minutes notice.

WAR DIARY
INTELLIGENCE SUMMARY

Army Form C. 2118.

July 1917

Place	Date	Hour	Summary of Events and Information	Remarks and references to Appendices
In the Field	1.8.17		ESQUERDES. The Battalion continued its series of training ins and arrived at the Village of ESQUERDES. On Sunday 1st July a Brigade Church Parade was held at ESTAIRES. Special arrangements were made for the entrainment of the troops, and a miniature Rifle Range was found a necessity at an early date. Work was continued on the stations of wells, a the usual training was carried out. On July 4th the Battn practised the attack over the prepared trenches working in co-operation with the Machine Gun Coy, Stokes Mortar Battery. The Brigadier held an interview with the officers taking part. Each Platoon was taken slowly over the ground representing its position in the attack, all points being thoroughly explained by the Platoon Commander. A Practice Brigade attack took place on July 7th. Tanks and contact aeroplanes taking part. The Lewis guns were represented by drums & very lights. Demonstrations were given in finding spots from on two occasions a Brigade Church Parade was held at QUELMES on Sunday July 15th followed by Sports open to all units of the Brigade. The Brigade attack was again practised on 2 further occasions.	

War Diary
of the
1/10 Liverpool R
for the period
1st July to 31st July
1917.

Army Form C. 2118.

WAR DIARY
or
INTELLIGENCE SUMMARY

(Erase heading not required.)

Instructions regarding War Diaries and Intelligence Summaries are contained in F. S. Regs., Part II. and the Staff Manual respectively. Title pages will be prepared in manuscript.

Place	Date	Hour	Summary of Events and Information	Remarks and references to Appendices
In the field	1/7/17		On the evening of the 14th June Battn was relieved by 2nd NORTHAMPTON. REGT, and on relief proceeded to cambch near VLAMERTINGHE, moving over the following evening to camp previously occupied (now called QUERY CAMP). MAJOR. J. L. A. MACDONALD was admitted to hospital the same evening, and LIEUT. B. ARKLE, M.C., returned from 166th Infantry Brigade H.Qrs (where he had been temporarily attached for instruction in staff duties) and re-assumed duties of adjutant. On June 18th orders were received that Battn would move on the following day, by train from POPERINGHE, to ZEGGERS-CAPPEL. These orders were duly carried out and Battn arrived at ZEGGERS-CAPPEL in the early evening, all being safely housed by 9. a.m. The following day, the Battn moved, at 10. a.m, by motor-lorries to ZUDAUSQUES, via ST OMER — the training being completed by 3. p.m. Training, and the digging of trenches were carried out daily until the 30th inst, when Battn (less 1 Coy) which remained behind for digging) moved into new billeting area at ESQUERDES leaving ZOUDASQUES at 7. a. m. & arriving in billets at 9. a. m. The company detailed for digging rejoined in the evening. Total Casualties for month. Officers 1 Wounded. O/Ranks {Killed 2 / Died of wounds 9 / Wounded 31} Total 42	

B. Alley
Lieut.
COMMANDING, 1/10th (SCOTTISH) BATTN. THE KINGS (LIVERPOOL REGT.)

LIEUT. COLONEL.

WAR DIARY
INTELLIGENCE SUMMARY

Army Form C. 2118.

June 1917

Place	Date	Hour	Summary of Events and Information	Remarks and references to Appendices
In the Field	1/7/17		On 1st June, the Battn (less two coys in YPRES) were billeted in "B" camp. On the evening of the 2nd the enemy shelled the camp causing some casualties. Consequent upon this, the Battn moved the following evening to a canvas camp near VLAMERTINGHE. On the night 5th June the companies in YPRES were relieved, and on relief moved to positions at MACHINE GUN FARM and L.8. POST. Working parties for the front line were supplied nightly by this detachment. On 11th June the whole Battn moved to relieve the 1/5 SOUTH LANCS REGT in RAILWAY WOOD sector, obtaining the position at 3. a. m. 12/15 June. On the following night a mine was blown out the lip of some consolidated by "V" & "X" Coys under the supervision of CAPT. L. G. WALL and 2nd LIEUT. A. GLEDSDALE. Only one casualty was sustained during the consolidation. The enemy fired small mines in the early hours of the following morning — no damage being done to our trenches, the surface of the ground being only just penetrated. Again, the following morning, the enemy fired one small mine on our left — no damage, four counterfeits being caused.	

CONFIDENTIAL

War Diary
of
1/10 Liverpool. R.
for the period
June 1st to June 30th, 1917.

WAR DIARY

INTELLIGENCE SUMMARY.

(Erase heading not required.)

Army Form C. 2118.

Summary of Events and Information

Place	Date	Hour	Summary of Events and Information	Remarks and references to Appendices
In the field	1/6/17		accordingly carried out the same evening. Working parties were supplied nightly from "B" Camp for work in front line trenches. On the 28th, another company was ordered to ECOLE, 1PR 65. Lt Col. J R DAVIDSON, C.M.G. returned from leave, and assumed command of the Battn, on 30th May.	

Total casualties for month:-

	Killed	Wounded
Officers	.	.
O/Ranks	3	19
Total.	3	19

J R Davidson
Lieut-Col Commdg
1/10th (Scottish) Bn. The King's (Liverpool Regt)

Place	Date	Hour	Summary of Events and Information	Remarks and references to Appendices
In Rufiji	11/6/17		On the night 18/19th May, Bn was relieved by 1/5 SOUTH LANCS REGT, and in turn relieved 1/4th K.L.R. in the POTIJZE sector – two companies remaining at CONVENT, YPRES for work.

The enemy was fairly quiet for the ensuing five days during which time working parties made considerable progress in repairing trenches etc.

Three officer Reinforcements reported for duty on May 21st.
On 25th May, the Battn 'side-stepped' to the right, one company holding front line, one company the support line and Battn Headquarters being located at DRAGOON FARM.
Battn was relieved on the 25th by 1/5 LOYAL NORTH LANCS REGT and on relief, proceeded (by tram from YPRES to BRANDHOEK) to 'B' Camp. One company was left at the CONVENT, YPRES to furnish working parties for the front line.
The following day, orders were received that one company would occupy L.4 POST, near YPRES. These orders were | |

Army Form C. 2118.

May 1917

WAR DIARY
INTELLIGENCE SUMMARY
(Erase heading not required.)

Instructions regarding War Diaries and Intelligence Summaries are contained in F.S. Regs., Part II. and the Staff Manual respectively. Title pages will be prepared in manuscript.

Places	Date	Hour	Summary of Events and Information	Remarks and references to Appendices
In Reties	1/6/17		Battn occupying trenches in the ST JEAN sector. On the night of 3rd May, Battn was relieved by the 1/5 LOYAL NORTH LANCS. REGT and on relief moved to billets in and about the PRISON, YPRES. Working parties were supplied both by day and night until the early morning of the 8th when Battn was relieved by the 1/5. LANCS. FUS. On relief, Battn marched to VLAMERTINGHE and entrained for POPERINGHE, thence marching to "Y" camp all being reported in by 7:30 a.m. On May 10th, the Brigadier-General Commdg 166th Infantry Brigade inspected the Battn in mass formation. Training was carried out on the usual lines – special attention being given to march discipline. The Battn entrained on May 17th at POPERINGHE and proceeded to YPRES, relieving the 1/5. KING'S OWN. ROYAL LANC. REGT in the ECOLE and surrounding billets. The same day Lieut.-Col. J.R. DAVIDSON. C.M.G. proceeded on leave to England – Major T.L.R. MACDONALD assuming command of the Battn	

T2134. Wt. W708–776. 500000. 4/15. Sir J. C. & S.

CONFIDENTIAL

War Diary
of
1/10th Liverpool R.
for the period
May 1st to 31st, 1917

Army Form C. 2118.

WAR DIARY
INTELLIGENCE SUMMARY.
(Erase heading not required.)

(3)

Place	Date	Hour	Summary of Events and Information	Remarks and references to Appendices
In the field	1/5/19		Total Casualties for month	

	Officers	O.Ranks	Total
Killed in action		7	7
Died of wounds		1	1
Wounded	2	20	22
			30

M. Davidson LIEUT. COLONEL
COMMANDING 10TH (SCOTTISH) BN. THE KING'S (LIVERPOOL REGT.)

WAR DIARY
or
INTELLIGENCE SUMMARY.

Army Form C. 2118.

Place	Date	Hour	Summary of Events and Information	Remarks and references to Appendices
In the field	1/5/17		The following night, Battn relieved 1/8th (IRISH) K.L.R. in the ST JEAN section - relief being carried out without loss. Lt Col. J R DAVIDSON and Major J L A MACDONALD left Battn the same day for a five days course at VIII Corps School. — Capt. L G WALL assuming command of the Battn. During the following five days the enemy shelled the trenches intermittently and his machine guns were active at nights. On the 22nd April, Battn was relieved by 1/5 LOYAL NORTH LANCS REGT and moved, on relief, to billets in and around the PRISON. Lt Col. J R DAVIDSON and Major J L A MACDONALD rejoined the Battn the same day. Working parties — necessitating all available men being called upon, were supplied daily for work on trenches etc. On the 26th, Capt. B ARKLE, M.C. left Battn to attend a course at the 2nd Army School, his duties of adjutant being temporarily taken over by 2Lt A J LYLE. The following day, Battn again relieved 1/5 LOYAL NORTH LANCS REGT in the ST JEAN sector, and at the close of the month were still in this position, having sustained only one casualty.	

April 1917

Army Form C. 2118.

WAR DIARY
INTELLIGENCE SUMMARY

(Erase heading not required.)

Instructions regarding War Diaries and Intelligence Summaries are contained in F.S. Regs., Part II. and the Staff Manual respectively. Title pages will be prepared in manuscript.

Place	Date	Hour	Summary of Events and Information	Remarks and references to Appendices
In the field	1/5/17		Battn in "C" Camp near BRANDHOEK. Usual training was carried out daily until the 6th April, when orders were received that Battn would relieve 1/9 K.L.R. at CONVENT billets in YPRES, the same evening. These orders were carried out, Battn proceeding by rail from BRANDHOEK to YPRES relief being completed at 10.30 p.m. The following day, the enemy shelled the billets occupied by a company of this Battn, causing several casualties. In the evening, the Battn relieved 1/7 K.L.R. in POTIJZE sector. The enemy was exceptionally quiet during the succeeding five days. Battn was relieved on the 12th, by 1/5 LOYAL NORTH LANCS REGT and on relief moved to YPRES, occupying previous billets in CONVENT AREA. Daily working parties were supplied from here - practically the whole Battn being engaged on these duties. On 14th April, Capt. H. R. KERR, A.S.C. joined Battn for attachment for one months instruction, prior to taking up a staff appointment. Battn proceeded to dugouts on CANAL BANK on the evening of the 16th, relieving the 1/4 K.O. ROYAL LANCS. REGT in this positions.	

CONFIDENTIAL

Vol 28

War Diary

of

1/10 Liverpool Regt.

for the period

April 1st to 30th 1917

Army Form C. 2118.

WAR DIARY
or
INTELLIGENCE SUMMARY

(Erase heading not required.)

Place	Date	Hour	Summary of Events and Information	Remarks and references to Appendices
In the field	1/4/17		On relief, 2 Coys remained in YPRES and one Coy moved by train to PROVEN for work under R.E. Remainder of Battn proceeded by train to BRANDHOEK and hence to "C" camp. The following day, Battn moved over to "C" camp. Training was carried out for the next three days, chiefly Lewis Gunners & Rifle Grenadiers and the new formations of a Platoon in the attack. Total Casualties for month:- 3 killed + 13 Wounded (died of Wounds)	

Commanding 10th (Scottish) Bn. The K.L.R. (LIVERPOOL REGT)

WAR DIARY

INTELLIGENCE SUMMARY

(Erase heading not required.)

Army Form C. 2118.

Place	Date	Hour	Summary of Events and Information	Remarks and references to Appendices
In the field	1/4/17		Capt A.G. DAVIDSON, M.C. rejoined the Battn today from England. The whole Battn was engaged on various R.E and other working parties during this period. On the night of the 16th, Battn moved over to billets in the PRISON for one night, and the following evening (17th) relieved 1/8 (IRISH) BATTN. K.L.R. in the ST JEAN sector. Relief was completed safely by 10.35 p.m. The enemy were more active during the next few days, using continually a new type of rifle grenade causing several casualties. There was also a considerable amount of activity behind the enemy's lines, transport and troops on the move being observed. On 23rd March 1/5 LOYAL NORTH LANCS REGT relieved the Battn. Battn moved on relief to billets in and about the PRISON, YPRES. Here the usual R.E and other working parties were supplied daily. On the 28th inst, the Battn was relieved by 2/5 LANCS FUSILIERS	

WAR DIARY
or
INTELLIGENCE SUMMARY

Army Form C. 2118.

March 1917

Place	Date	Hour	Summary of Events and Information	Remarks and references to Appendices
In the field	1/4/17		Battn in "C" Camp. Daily training was carried out until March 5th when orders were received that Battn would move up the line the following evening. These orders were duly carried out and Battn entrained at BRANDHOEK and moved to YPRES, occupying cellars at CONVENT DES CARMES and surrounding billets. On 48 inst Battn relieved 1/4 K.L.R. in the POTIJZE sector, relief being completed without casualties. The Battn remained in this sector until the 12th, during which time the enemy was fairly quiet except for an occasional minenwerfer. Work was carried on repairing this trenches, thickening the parapets, building up paradoses etc. On 12th inst, Lt Col. J. R. DAVIDSON left Battn to be attached for 48 hours to a Heavy Battery, the command of the Battn being taken over by Major. J. L. A. MACDONALD. The same evening the Battn was relieved by 1/5 LOYAL NORTH LANCS, & on relief marched to CONVENT & billets in YPRES. Lt Col J R DAVIDSON returned to Battn on 14th and assumed command.	

War Diary
of the
1/10 Liverpool Regt
for the period
1st to 31st March
1917.

Army Form C. 2118.

WAR DIARY or INTELLIGENCE SUMMARY

(Erase heading not required.)

Place	Date	Hour	Summary of Events and Information	Remarks and references to Appendices
Field	1/3/17		From 25th inst. the new composition of the Battn. was brought into force, according to orders from G.H.Q. The Battn. was relieved on the 25th Feb. by 1/4 LOYAL NORTH LANCS, and moved on relief, to "C" Camp near BRANDHOEK, by train from YPRES, all being reported in billets by 11.45 P.M. The following day was given over to cleaning up generally, towing being provided with on the 3rd inst. Special attention being paid to the new composition of the Battalion in the attack.	

Casualties for the month.

	Officers	o/Ranks
Killed + Died of Wounds	—	6
Wounded	—	5

Roy Alley
Capt. Adjt.

(LIEUT. COLONEL,
COMMANDING 10TH (SERVICE) BATTN. THE KING'S (LIVERPOOL REGT.)

Army Form C. 2118.

WAR DIARY
or
INTELLIGENCE=SUMMARY

(Erase heading not required.)

(2)

Place	Date	Hour	Summary of Events and Information	Remarks and references to Appendices
field	1/2/17		to YPRES, thence marching to CANAL BANK dugouts and relieving 1st CAMBRIDGESHIRE REGT. The Coy that had been temporarily attached to the 14th R.W.F. rejoined the Battn here and reported that they had sustained casualties as follows:- 6 killed 5 wounded - during their period of attachment. The following evening, Battn relieved 1/1 HERTS REGT in the line, relief being completed at 10 p.m. ST JEAN sector of the line. Battn occupied this position for the next five days. Owing to the poor visibility, the Artillery on both sides was very quiet & no casualties were sustained. On 18th Feb. LT. COL. J.R. DAVIDSON left the Battn to attend a six days course at the 2nd Army School, and MAJOR J L A MACDONALD (2nd in command) assumed command of the Battn. On the night of the 20th Feb., Battn was relieved by the 1/5. LOYAL NORTH LANCS, and on relief proceeded to CANAL BANK dugouts. Here, large fatigues were supplied daily, practically every man being called upon. LT COL. F.W.M.DREW (who after handing over to Lt Col. J.R.DAVIDSON) returned, and went to Divisional H.Q.°, ~~the following day~~ in accordance with instructions received by him. Lt Col. J.R. DAVIDSON rejoined the Battn this day from 2nd Army School and took over command from MAJOR J L A MASDONALD.	

Army Form C. 2118.

WAR DIARY
or
INTELLIGENCE SUMMARY
(Erase heading not required.)

February 1917

Place	Date	Hour	Summary of Events and Information	Remarks and references to Appendices
Field	1/3/17		On 1st Feb the Battalion was at BOLLEZEELE in Divisional Reserve where training was carried out daily. Orders were received on the 2nd that Battn would move to new area on the following day. Movement orders were received later and accordingly on the morning of the 3rd, Battn entrained at BOLLEZEELE and proceeded to POPERINGHE, where detrainment was carried out and Battn marched by platoons to MOUTON FARM (near ELVERDINGHE) relieving the 2/5 LANCS. FUSILIERS. You next six days, daily fatigues were supplied and company training carried out. On 5th Feb Lt Col J. R. DAVIDSON rejoined the command. On 9th Feb Battn was relieved by 1/5 SOUTH LANCS REGT & moved on relief to "E" Camp. A draft of 167 O/Ranks joined Battn this day from England, which was sent to the Divisional Reinforcement Camp for further training. Orders were received that one company of 5 Officers and 114 O/Ranks was to be attached to 14th Battn R.W.F. in the line. Consequently, the required numbers was sent off the same day and duly reported to 14th R W Fs at CANAL BANK dug outs. The usual training was proceeded with, and a few fatigue parties supplied daily. On 15th Feb Battn entrained at BRANDHOEK & proceeded	

CONFIDENTIAL

War Diary
of
1/10th Liverpool Regt
for the period
1st to 28th February 1917.

WAR DIARY or INTELLIGENCE SUMMARY

Army Form C. 2118.

Place	Date	Hour	Summary of Events and Information	Remarks and references to Appendices

Ys same day at 1 p.m. the Bathn. moved to ST. OMER & MARKET POPERINGHE arriving at 2 p.m. and entrained for the Narrow Gauge railway for BULLASSELE where billets were occupied. The following days were spent in the Specialists training of Companies & specialists, which on many days had to be carried out in very inclement weather, a course being set on the 19th and lasts to the end of the month. A Bridge near SOMME TOWN YARD took place on the 20th all ranks taking part. The Brigade carried out special training in "Attack" and Deployment prior to an attack, a Section of the Machine Gun Coy being allotted to each Battalion, the attack from Trench to Trench was also practised by the Brigade.

A cross country run took place on the 28th by teams representing each Battalion in the Brigade, a prize being offered by the Brigadier General which was won by the 1/5 South Lancs.

The G.O.C. 55 Div. inspected the Battalion on the 29th whilst carrying on close order drill & bayonet fighting, two in progress.

During the month the following officers were awarded the Military Cross by His Majesty the King:— Capt. A. CARLE & Capt. G.D. MORTON, for distinguished service in the Field, also mentioned in Dispatches:- Lt Col. R. DAVIDSON & Lt Col. F.W.M. DREW (attached to 5 Lanc. Regt.) & Col. C.P. JAMES who in a considerable time was adjutant of the Battn.

Lt. E.R. GLAZEBROOK Rgt Sgt. Major S. JENNINGS, Sgt. E. GAYNARD

TOTAL CASUALTIES FOR MONTH Killed — 1
                               Wounded — 4
                               "at duty" — 18

F.M. Drew
Lieut. Colonel
Commanding 1/8th (Scottish) Bn the Kings (Liverpool Regt)

WAR DIARY
or
INTELLIGENCE SUMMARY.

Report ofter a Bombardment lasting 125 minutes 2 Parties from 1/5 L.N.Lancs raised a party of the enemy trench opposite that held by the Battalion in spite of a heavy retaliatory bombardment on the part of the enemy, no casualties occurred and the portion due was limited to the above mentioned bombardment. The trenches were found to have been largely damaged and completely avoidable man was killed out to bits the work which was extensively continued was entirely useless. Some heavy shelling was experienced on our front line also on our left our artillery replies very effectively. During the afternoon of the 12th when relief by the 11 yorks was nearing completion the enemy put a very heavy Barrage of minenwerfer on our front line also on that of the Battn. on our right. Not Battn Sent up S.O.S signal about the same time, and a very fine example of the enemy's trench followed but to no purpose as no further attack of any kind appeared.

Casualties during 11/12 + 12/13 were 11 killed + 1 officer slightly wounded. Relief was finally completed at 11.45 p.m. and (B.Coy Queens) to Ypres & entrained there for BEDNINGHAM and Remainder at B Camp. Trains & Monmouth by the 13th. Completions to the transport sector the next day. Lt. Col. F.M.M. DREW returned from Leave BOESINGHE + assumed Command of the Battalion on the 14th.

A.5834 Wt.W.4973/M687/ 750,000 8/16 D.D.& L.Ltd. Forms/C.2118/13.

WAR DIARY or INTELLIGENCE SUMMARY

January 1917

Place: Le Transloy
Date: January 1917

On Jan 1st 2 Companies were in the front line, 1 in support and 1 in the village under the Command of Capt B. Orkle in the temporary absence of the O.C. 2 W.N. Drews. A considerable amount of hostile shelling took place on the left of our position a few still also falling in the village. The Battalion were relieved on the following day by 1/5 L. North Lancs and moved to the Camp Rules Dug-out. Jan 3rd fatigues and working parties were supplied from the Battn. Jan 4th the enemy sights a small party of the 1/9 R.S. LANCS in DURHAM Trench carried a section of 1/9R trench by surprise also following day the Battn relieved scaries on the Rules Dead End of camel Pr, Jan 5th the Battn relieved the 1/4 N Hamp to the same position as that held on the 1st and occupies a sector to the eastward. (J) enemy shells a directly in front of Right Sector on 6th above was killed. Early the morning of 7th orderly the Coys commenced to be attacked by the Germans preceded by the Battn HQ and officers Bombs and the B. including the Bullet J. NOs and Tokes were cut off, when P. stn over Rt 45 one Lieut Curtis and 30 were in a miscellaneous attempt to get rid of such a mass and above were quite forces till. In the attempt ^ the game, including dead were believed that the whole of the 2 lost Lieut land stone to prevent the tramping of to MIELFE. The Bn were out at 3pm and it took until 10.30am. to...

Vol 25

War Diary

of the

1/10 Liverpool R

for the period

1/1/17 to 31/1/17.

Army Form C. 2118.

WAR DIARY
INTELLIGENCE SUMMARY

(Erase heading not required.)

Instructions regarding War Diaries and Intelligence Summaries are contained in F. S. Regs, Part II. and the Staff Manual respectively. Title Pages will be prepared in manuscript.

Place	Date	Hour	Summary of Events and Information	Remarks and references to Appendices
Inkefield	1/1/17		Total Casualties for month of December 1916.	

	Killed	Wounded	Total
Officers	-	-	-
O/Ranks	4	10	14

Grand Total 14

Army Form C. 2118.

WAR DIARY
INTELLIGENCE SUMMARY
(Erase heading not required.)

Place	Date	Hour	Summary of Events and Information	Remarks and references to Appendices
In the field	1/1/17.		in his name for all the good work the Battn. had done for him in the past and recently. On the 23rd inst. the G.O.C. 2nd Army inspected the Battn, and he also congratulated the Battn particularly on its very fine Success in the raid undertaken on the 29th ult. and on its good work generally, and told the Commdg officer & the officers that it was their duty to teach all ranks joining, what a fine Battn. they had come to. Ordinary training was carried out daily until the 27th inst., with the exception of Christmas Day, which was a general holiday, except for one parade, on which Xmas gifts, given by the Officers relatives, were distributed by the Commdg Officer. Orders were received on the evening of the 26th, that the Battn would move up the line the following afternoon. Later these orders were confirmed and consequently Battn moved by train to YPRES on the 27th and relieved the 2/5. LANCS FUSILIERS. in CANAL BANK dugouts in the late afternoon the following day, Battn relieved the 1/8 (IRISH) K.L.R. in the ST JEAN - WIELTJE section. On the 31st Dec. the Commdg officer being away on a course, CAPT. B. ARKIE took over command of the Battn.	

Army Form C. 2118.

WAR DIARY
or
INTELLIGENCE SUMMARY
(Erase heading not required.)

(2)

Instructions regarding War Diaries and Intelligence Summaries are contained in F. S. Regs., Part II. and the Staff Manual respectively. Title Pages will be prepared in manuscript.

Place	Date	Hour	Summary of Events and Information	Remarks and references to Appendices
In the field	1/1/17.		A draft of 43 o/Ranks reported for duty today. Again the following day enemy heavily shelled our front line, doing a great deal of damage. Hard work was necessary to clean the trench, but this was done the same night, and the Brigadier expressed himself very pleased with the result and the way the men had worked to clean the trench. CAPT. L. G. WALL rejoined Battn today from ENGLAND and took over command of "V" Coy. On the evening of the 18th inst., Battn was relieved by the 2/5. LANCS. FUSILIERS. (everything being complete by 6.40 p.m.) and marched to YPRES station, where Battn entrained for BRANDHOEK, from where Battn marched to "C" Camp, all being reported in by 10.30 p.m. It was understood that the COMMANDER-IN-CHIEF would inspect the Battn on the 19th inst but orders were afterwards received that the inspection would take place on the 21st. The intervening time being spent in cleaning up generally and refitting. As the 21st turned out very wet, the C.in C. inspected the men outside their huts, also the camp, and complimented the Commdg Officer on a very fine Battn and asked the Commdg Officer to thank the Battn	

WAR DIARY or INTELLIGENCE SUMMARY

December 1916

Place	Date	Hour	Summary of Events and Information	Remarks and references to Appendices
In the field	1/1/17		Battn in dugouts on CANAL BANK, YPRES. On the evening of the 1st inst Battn relieved the 1/5 LOYAL NORTH LANCS. REGT in the usual sector ST JEAN, WIELTJE etc - relief being completed without a hitch by 7.20 pm. The trenches were in fairly good condition, but in parts had been blown in, which necessitated fatigue parties being detailed to repair same. The following five days were spent in work on the trenches, improving etc special attention being paid to the barbed wire entanglements, a party of 2 NCO's + 24 men was detailed to work on this nightly. During this tour the enemy was very quiet. On Dec 6th word was received that 3 O/Ranks had been awarded the MILITARY MEDAL for gallantry in the work under taken by this Battn on the 29th ult. On Dec 7th Battn was relieved by 1/5. LOYAL NORTH LANCS REGT, & on relief marched back to dugouts on CANAL BANK. Here, the usual fatigue parties were supplied by day and by night, practically the whole Battn being engaged on fatigue duties. A wire was received on the 10th inst notifying the Battn of the award of the MILITARY CROSS to 2nd Lt. R. V. CLARK for gallantry on Nov 29th. The usual periodical relief was carried out on the 12th inst, the Battn relieving the 1/5. LOYAL NORTH LANCS in the ST JEAN - WIELTJE sector. Enemy artillery was inactive until the 14th inst, when it opened out on BILGE TRENCH, blowing in the trench, but luckily causing only three slight casualties.	

CONFIDENTIAL

Vol 24

War Diary

of

1/10th Liverpool Regt

for period

December 1st to 31st 1916

55th Division No. 850/6 (3)

55th Division 'G'.

PRELIMINARY REPORT ON RAID ON GERMAN TRENCHES.

The barrage started punctually. A few 18-pdr. shells fell short but this was soon rectified. Nobody was hit in the Crater where the parties were assembled, either by our own shells or the enemy's.

At ZERO - 30 the Torpedoes in our own wire were exploded.

At ZERO the parties were marshalled and got away quickly. Progress was slow as the ground was very heavy and wet.

At ZERO plus 15 three wounded men came back and a little later four prisoners, who were immediately sent down under escort to Brigade. At Zero plus 30, the bugles were blown and the parties began to return, together with some other prisoners, when it appeared that Lieut. MOSS Commanding the Right Party had been killed and that Lieut. COLLEY was reported missing, believed killed; Two riflemen are known to have been killed and there are about 10 wounded. Three are still missing but are being searched for.

Progress in enemy trenches was slow owing to the very effective work of our artillery which is said to have complete-ly obliterated enemy trenches, making them quite unrecog--nisable. Three dugouts bombed - three German dead seen in trench - four Germans killed by our men - two German prisoners killed returning to our trenches.

German trenches about 7 feet deep, sandbagged, revetted with fascines and brushwood, floorboarded, slightly wet.

(Signed) F.J.DUNCAN,
Brigadier-General
29th November 16.   Commanding 165th Infantry Brigade.

-2-

VIIIth Corps.

The above 'Preliminary Report on Raid on German Trenches' by 165th Infantry Brigade is forwarded.

55th Division H.Q.,
29th November 1916.
Major-General
Commanding 55th Division.

Two concrete dugouts badly blown about were found at extreme point of KAISER BILL.

Bugler sounding signal for recall distinctly heard, also pause in our barrage.

Tapes previously laid guided party to our trenches.

All parties report that KAISER BILL was filled with wire in every direction, and much blown about.

The time allowed did not prove sufficient to thoroughly explore all the trenches.

It is quite possible that enemy wire on South side of KAISER BILL was cut by trench mortars but it was not found and therefore torpedo was used.

No machine guns or trench mortars were found.

Some equipment and papers found were taken.

Our bombardment appears to have been most effective except on the front trench on Southern side of salient.

The Stokes Mortars were ready to fire according to programme but at 4.30 p.m. an enemy shell dropped in C.29.5. and buried two guns and ammunition.

At 4.35 p.m. fire was opened at an increased rate to make up for the loss of two guns, and it appeared most effective.

10 Vickers guns fired according to programme.

8 prisoners were captured, one of them wounded. *in addition to those killed*

29/11/1916.

BRIGADIER GENERAL.
Commanding 166 Infantry Brigade.

Trench about 8 feet deep, well boarded, very little knocked about by shelling, revetted with fascines on each side; no fire step.

Two dugouts found near junction with support line. A bomb was thrown in and two Germans gave themselves up.

Party proceeded along trench being fired at from some distance off with rifles. One man of party wounded.

One German shot in a dugout.

Signal for withdrawal heard easily, also bugle in our trench. Parties were checked coming out of trench through gap in wire and were guided back to our trench by two tapes previously laid.

An electric lamp that was placed in right gap of enemy's wire turned towards KAISER BILL to guide right party out drew enemy's fire, and was quickly knocked out.

The left party found enemy wire at C.29.a.90.04 excellently cut and a broad gap through it.

At 5 p.m. left party entered trench and proceeded according to programme.

Trenches very much knocked about and progress very slow. Trenches generally 7 feet deep, 3 feet wide, revetted with fascines, and floorboarded.

Right forward party proceeded without opposition to support line and turned to the right and came on a dugout divided into three compartments made of reinforced concrete. Bombs were thrown from these dugouts. Our men threw in bombs and shouted to the Germans to come out. Three gave themselves up. The dugout was blown up by Engineers before withdrawal.

The Left Clearing Party met with opposition from enemy at junction of Support Line with main communication trench. Our men bombed them and used their rifles and bayonets. 8 Germans gave themselves up and were sent back to gap.

It was them time to come out. A good many 4.2 were falling in the salient, and one wounded the escort to prisoners and killed some of prisoners.

Engineer party blew up a concrete dugout and some kind of gun emplacement on withdrawing.

The left clearing party came across a shell hole and bombs were thrown from it. A Stokes mortar bomb was thrown into it and no more bombs were thrown.

The left bombing and blocking party followed front line trench on North-East side of KAISER BILL to junction of Support Line, and formed block but met with no enemy to their deep regret.

10th Liverpool Nov 1916.   15

55th Division.

Reference Trench Map ST. JULIEN -
28.N.W.2. 1/10,000 Edition 3.A.

PRELIMINARY REPORT ON RAID UNDERTAKEN BY THE
10th LIVERPOOL SCOTTISH on the
29th November 1916.

PLACE.   KAISER BILL.

NARRATIVE OF RAID.

The raiding party left the CANAL BANK at 2.30 p.m. and proceeded via ST. JEAN Road to Junction Road. Here, the right raiding party, 1 Officer and 30 other ranks proceeded via POTIJZE and the HAYMARKET communication trench to the front line and got into position at 3.45 p.m.

The left raiding party, 2 officers, 42 other ranks proceeded via GARDEN STREET and NEW JOHN STREET and got into position at 3.40 p.m.

The trenches within 300 yards of KAISER BILL had previously been cleared to allow Heavy Artillery to fire without danger to men in front line trench.

At 4.40 p.m. Heavy Artillery lifted and both raiding parties moved into position facing KAISER BILL. In doing so 4 men were wounded.

A good deal of shelling by 4.2 and 5.9 and trench mortars had taken place after our bombardment commenced, and our trench was badly blown in, two of the torpedoes belonging to the left party being buried.

At 4.45 p.m. the parties got over our parapet and went through gaps in our wire and formed up ready to move.

At 4.50 p.m. both raiding parties advanced.

Very little fire of any kind was brought to bear on them. The right party was delayed by shells bursting in front of them, whether our own barrage or German seems uncertain, most probably latter.

The right party was unable to find a gap at C.29.c.95.98 so a torpedo was brought up and fired. The wire was well cut, and party entered in good order and followed trench to the East in front line.

1.

WAR DIARY
INTELLIGENCE SUMMARY.
(Erase heading not required.)

Army Form C. 2118.

Place	Date	Hour	Summary of Events and Information	Remarks and references to Appendices
In Field	1/12/16		Total Casualties for the month	
			Officers O.Ranks	
			Killed — 5 (1 accidentally)	
			Missing — 1	
			Wounded 3 (2 accidentally) 36 (11 accidentally)	
			3 42	

[signature] LIEUT. COLONEL,
COMMANDING 10TH (SCOTTISH) BN THE KING'S (L'POOL REGT.)

WAR DIARY / INTELLIGENCE SUMMARY

Army Form C. 2118.

Place	Date	Hour	Summary of Events and Information	Remarks and references to Appendices
In the field	1/7/16		2 Officers Reinforcements joined the Battn this day. As arranged, the raid took place on the 29th inst. After a preliminary bombardment by the Field Artillery, the Heavy Artillery opened up and fired on the objective — KAISER BILL — for about 20 minutes. At 4.50 p.m. the raiding party (which was divided into two parties) advanced to the assault and entered the German trenches at KAISER BILL and proceeded to carry out the programme previously arranged. The raid was a great success and much useful information and identifications were obtained. Also, eight prisoners were actually brought into our lines, five others being killed on the way back. The Divisional General inspected the Raiding parties the following day and congratulated them and the Battn on the results of the raid. Thus considering, by the enemy artillery were fairly heavy. The day of the 30th was spent during fatigue duty, all available men being employed.	

Place	Date	Hour	Summary of Events and Information	Remarks and references to Appendices
In the field	11/2/16		The Battn. on relief, entrained at YPRES & proceeded to BRANDHOEK, eventually arriving at "C" camp about midnight. The following eight days were spent in training. A raiding party was continually practising a proposed raid which was to be undertaken by this Battn. on a salient in the enemy's lines. A most unfortunate accident occurred on the 22nd inst. while the raiding party was practising live bomb-throwing, a bomb exploded instantaneously killing 1 O'Rank and injuring 2 Officers and 11 O'Ranks. A board of Enquiry was held the following day, in which it was found that the accident could not have been avoided in any way and the whole thing being due to a faulty bomb. Orders were received on the 24th inst that the raid would impact the Battn the following day, but these orders were subsequently cancelled, as the day turned out very wet. On Nov 29th Battn marched off at 4 p.m. and entrained at YPRES and detraining, Battn marched to dugouts on CANAL BANK, relieving the 1/5 LOYAL NORTH LANCS in this position and also two platoons in the LA BRIQUE POST. Nov 28th was the day fixed for the raid, but owing to misty weather, the raid was postponed till the following day.	

November 1916.

WAR DIARY
INTELLIGENCE SUMMARY

Army Form C. 2118.

Place	Date	Hour	Summary of Events and Information	Remarks and references to Appendices
In the field	1/12/16		From Nov 1st to Nov 8th the Battn was in dugouts on CANAL BANK, YPRES. Fatigue parties were supplied daily for work on the front line, & cable-communication. On Nov 8th Battn relieved the 1/5 LOYAL NORTH LANCS REGT. in front line and support trenches, Battn HQr being situated in ST JEAN. One company was also in ST JEAN in reserve. The trenches were in none too good a state and hard work was necessary in order to make them tenable. The Commdg officer (LIEUT. COL. E W M DREW) went on leave this night, the command of the Battn being taken over by the Adjutant - CAPT. B. ARKLE - 2nd LT. C B EWART acting adjutant in the meantime. On Nov. 10 a new scheme for the defence of WIELTJE was received and consequently the following day, dispositions were made accordingly. The Divisional Commander visited the sector occupied by this Battn on Nov 12. The same day an inter-regimental relief took place, the companies in the front line being relieved by those in support and reserve. During this time the enemy artillery was very quiet, but on Nov 14th, owing to the good visibility, it became very active and shelled our trenches heavily, but causing only three casualties. On Nov. 16 the Corps Commdr & Divisional Commdr visited the trenches occupied by this Battn and expressed themselves highly satisfied with everything they saw, both as regards the work in hand and the cleanliness of the trenches and men. The 1/8th (IRISH) BN K.L.R relieved the Battn on Nov. 18, relief being complete at 8 p.m.	

53/166

Vol 23

CONFIDENTIAL

War Diary
of
1/10th Liverpool Regt
for period
1st November to 30th ~~September~~ November 1916

Army Form C. 2118.

WAR DIARY
INTELLIGENCE SUMMARY
(Erase heading not required.)

Place	Date	Hour	Summary of Events and Information	Remarks and references to Appendices
In the field	2/11/16		TOTAL CASUALTIES FOR MONTH	
			OFFICERS O/RANKS TOTAL	
			KILLED 1 9 10	
			WOUNDED 2 45 47	
			[signature] LIEUT. COLONEL, COMMANDING 10TH (SERVICE) Bn THE KING'S (LIVERPOOL REGT.)	

WAR DIARY
INTELLIGENCE SUMMARY

(Erase heading not required.)

Army Form C. 2118.

Place	Date	Hour	Summary of Events and Information	Remarks and references to Appendices
In the field	2/11/16		On the night of the 18th Oct., while a party was working on front-line trench, the enemy opened up a heavy bombardment, causing 24 casualties in the Battn. The Battn. was relieved on the 23rd inst by 1/8 K.L.R. and marching off late in the afternoon relieved 1/9. K.L.R. in the ELVERDINGHE CHATEAU and "L" defence line. Battn. was disposed of as follows:- 2 Companies in CHATEAU, 1 Coy in L2 and L4 Posts, and 1 Company in L 8 Post. Three officer reinforcements reported for duty, being attached from 5th & 6th Battns ARGYLE & SUTHERLAND HIGHLANDERS. On 28th Oct. the medical officer of this Battn (CAPT. N.G. CHEVASSE, M.C.) received intimation that he had been awarded the VICTORIA CROSS for gallantry and devotion to duty on August 9th, 1916, during the attack on GUILLEMONT. The Battn. was in this position till 30th inst. and supplying fatigue parties daily to work for R.E., and also in improving defences. On 30th Oct. 1/4. K.O. ROYAL LANCASTER REGT. relieved the Battn. at ELVERDINGHE CHATEAU and in the "L" defences. Battn. on relief, marched to "C" camp near BRANDHOEK. The following day(s), orders were received that 1/5. LOYAL NORTH LANCS. REGT. would be relieved by this Battn. in dugouts on CANAL BANK, YPRES. The evening, Battn. moved off at 3 PM, relief being complete at 10. PM.	

WAR DIARY
INTELLIGENCE SUMMARY
(Erase heading not required.)

Army Form C. 2118.

Place	Date	Hour	Summary of Events and Information	Remarks and references to Appendices
In the field	2/11/16		Trenches and communication trenches, which were in bad condition owing to the weather, and needed constant attention & hard work to keep them in anything like good condition. On the 8th inst, the Brigadier-General Commanding informed the Commanding Officer that we would provide 5 Off & 150 O/Ranks to 8th CORPS HQrs to furnish guards etc. Subsequently, these orders were cancelled. The enemy shelled the front line trenches intermittently during the day. A draft of 5 Offrs arrived today from ENGLAND. On Oct. 9th enemy again shelled our trenches at intervals with minenwerfers causing several casualties. The two Companies in the front line were relieved by the two Companies in supports and reserve, relief being complete at 8 p.m. On Oct. 10th, the Brigadier General ordered that 1 platoon from the front line should return to outposts, thereby reducing the number of casualties caused by minenwerfers during daylight. Work was carried on during the next three days as usual and a vast improvement made on the trenches. Baths were received on the 13th inst by the 1/5. LOYAL NORTH LANCS REGT. and marched to dugouts on CANAL BANK (1 platoon occupying LA BRIQUE POST. The following eight days were spent in this position, the Battn supplying fatigue parties daily for cable-burying work on the front line, etc, etc.	

WAR DIARY
INTELLIGENCE SUMMARY

October 1916

Place	Date	Hour	Summary of Events and Information	Remarks and references to Appendices
In the field	2/11/16		Oct 1st Battn in billets in PONT-REMY. The Battn paraded in the afternoon and the Brigadier-General Commanding 166th Inf. Bgde decorated the men who had been awarded honours, for gallantry during the recent operations, which were as follows:- 4 Distinguished Conduct Medals and 6 Military Medals. Orders were received in the evening that Battn would, on the following day, march to ABBEVILLE, + there entrain for PROVEN, BELGIUM. Orders were issued accordingly + Battn paraded at 2 P.M. on the 2nd, marched to ABBEVILLE, entraining there and leaving ABBEVILLE at 5.45 P.M. On arrival at PROVEN at 5.10 AM the following morning, Battn marched to "K" Camp, POPERINGHE. Early the same afternoon orders were received that Battn would move to YPRES, the evening Parade was ordered for 4.30 P.M. and Battn marched off at that hour to POPERINGHE STATION, where Battn entrained for YPRES. Battn detrained near ASYLUM, YPRES and marched to dugouts on CANAL BANK, relieving the 1st Bn BORDER REGT in this position. The following night Battn relieved 1st/4th SOUTH WALES BORDERERS in front line trenches in front of WIELTZE, with Battn HQrs and one Coy in reserve in ST JEAN village. Battn in LA BRIQUE POST. All reliefs were completed by 8.40 p.m. The period Oct 5th Oct 8th the Battn worked very hard on the	

CONFIDENTIAL

Vol 20

55/cc
22

22 L

War Diary
of
1/10th (Scottish) Liverpool Regt
for the period
1st to 31st October 1916

WAR DIARY
INTELLIGENCE SUMMARY

Army Form C. 2118.

Place	Date	Hour	Summary of Events and Information	Remarks and references to Appendices
In the field	1/10/16		digging during the last few days & attributed a great part of the success of the assault by 165th Brigade to this fort in their attack. A party of 2 officers & 100 O.R.s who were sent on the night of the 26th to carry stretchers for O/C 1/3rd WEST LANCS FIELD AMBULANCE. Party arrived back in camp the following morning. On the 29th, the Brigadier came round & informed the Commanding Officer that 5 D.C.M's & 1 MILITARY CROSS had been awarded to the Battn for gallantry on Aug 9th. The following morning the Battn moved off to new billeting area at RIBEMONT, arriving there in the afternoon at 1.30pm. On the 29th orders were received that Battn would proceed by train to LONGPRE the following day. Accordingly, on the 30th, the Battn entrained at MERICOURT at 4.30am & arrived at LONGPRE at 8.15pm, where Battn detrained & marched to PONT-REMY to bivouac in a field.	

TOTAL CASUALTIES FOR MONTH

	Officers	of Ranks	Total
KILLED	1	21	22
WOUNDED	2	97	99
MISSING	-	3	3
			124

WAR DIARY
INTELLIGENCE SUMMARY

Army Form C. 2118.

Place	Date	Hour	Summary of Events and Information	Remarks and references to Appendices
In the field	11/10/16		In the field on Aug 9th, congratulated the recipients in the name of the G.O.C. 55th DIVISION, as well as himself. At 1 AM on the 18th the Battn. fell in & marched to SWITCH TRENCH & relieved the 10th Battn. ROYAL WEST KENT REGT. In the evening a warning order was received that Battn. would move up to support Trenches on EAST edge of FLERS village & relieve a Battn. of the 165th Brigade. Later, more orders were received & Battn. relieved 1/6th K.L.R. in the trenches - FOSSE WAY & FLERS AVENUE, relief being completed at 4 AM. During this period, the weather was very wet. Work was carried on the following night digging & deepening a new communication trench. The next morning the G.O.C. congratulated Battn. on work done the previous night, & issued orders to deepen & widen the new communication trench still more. Enemy artillery was very active & shelled our trenches heavily, causing some casualties. A party of 200 of Ranks reported to O.C. 1/5 K.O.R.L in the evening in order to dig & make fit for occupation a new front line trench. On the night of the 23rd Battn. were relieved by 1/6. K.L.R. on completion of relief at 12.40 AM marched to bivouac near POMMIER REDOUBT. The remainder of the day was given to the men to clean up. Three drafts of 110 of Ranks in all (including 40 details) joined this days. The G.O.C. DIVISION congratulated 166th BRIGADE on their splendid	

Army Form C. 2118.

WAR DIARY
or
INTELLIGENCE SUMMARY 3

(Erase heading not required.)

Instructions regarding War Diaries and Intelligence Summaries are contained in F.S. Regs., Part II. and the Staff Manual respectively. Title Pages will be prepared in manuscript.

Place	Date	Hour	Summary of Events and Information	Remarks and references to Appendices
In the field	1/10/16		The Battn moved to new camping area near RIBEMONT, arriving at camp in the early afternoon, where drafts of 1 Officer & 138 O/Ranks, who had been left behind for training at Divisional HQrs rejoined Battn. The period Sept 12-16 was given over to training, special attention being directed to practicing the attack by coys. A draft of 12 officers joined the Battn on the 13th inst being reinforcements from 4th (Res) Battn Q.O. CAMERON HIGHLANDERS, to which Regiment this Battn is affiliated, & were posted to their units for duration of the war. On the afternoon of the 16th inst, Battn moved to new bivouac area, at short notice, near ALBERT. During the night, orders were received that Battn would stand by ready to move at a moment's notice & at 11.15am further orders were received that Battn would move up to the trenches in fighting order. - Commanding Officers & all O.C. coys going up at 4 AM to view the trenches to be taken over. A draft of 40 O/Ranks arrived today. Authority was given for MAJOR F.W.M. DREW to wear the badges of Lieut-Col pending notification of same in LONDON GAZETTE. Battn paraded at 2.10pm & moved to POMMIER REDOUBT. On arrival here, orders were received that Battn would wait at this spot until midnight. The Brigadier General informed the Battn that 8 O/Ranks had been awarded the MILITARY MEDAL for distinguished conduct	

Army Form C. 2118.

WAR DIARY
INTELLIGENCE SUMMARY
(Erase heading not required.)

Instructions regarding War Diaries and Intelligence Summaries are contained in F. S. Regs., Part II and the Staff Manual respectively. Title Pages will be prepared in manuscript.

Place	Date	Hour	Summary of Events and Information	Remarks and references to Appendices
In the field	1/10/16		The following day the Battn relieved the 1st NORTH STAFFORDSHIRE REGT in Reserve trenches, MONTAUBAN, with two Coys & Battn of ROYAL FUSILIERS with remaining two Coys, which being completed at 4.30 P.M. The 6th inst was spent by all ranks in cleaning up the Trenches and surroundings. On the morning of the 7th, two Coys were relieved by 1st SOUTH STAFFS REGT, + came into Trenches near Battn H.Q.s. In the evening, all available men were turned out to dig strong points in front of front line N. end of DELVILLE WOOD. These were completed, & the strong points garrisoned by Battn. Remainder of the Battn returned to 'Reserve Trenches'. On the night of the 8th, all available men again went up to the front line & connected up the strong points dug the previous evening, & on completion occupied the new trench - now the front line - + at the same time running 1/5 Kings Own R.L. Regt. who went back to our trench at MONTAUBAN. Work during the following two days was carried on - salvage parties working through DELVILLE WOOD, burying dead, & digging in front line support line & deepening communication trenches. On Sept 10th orders were received that Battn would be relieved early the next morning by 23rd MIDDLESEX REGT. The Battn, after a hand over, being relieved by 23rd MIDDLESEX REGT, relief being completed at 5.35 AM on the 11th inst. Battn moved, on relief, to transport lines, after a halt for breakfast	

September 1916
WDO

WAR DIARY
INTELLIGENCE SUMMARY.
(Erase heading not required.)

Army Form C. 2118.

Hour, Date, Place	Summary of Events and Information	Remarks and references to Appendices
In the field 1-10-16	The Battalion in camp & bivouacs near MEAULTE. On the 1st inst Battn received orders to relieve 1st NORTH STAFFORDSHIRE REGT in Reserve trenches in front of MONTAUBAN on the night of the 2nd inst. The following afternoon these orders were cancelled & the Commanding Officer was informed that the major General required some night digging practised also relief of trenches & trench discipline as instructions for the new drafts. Training was duly carried out the same evening. At 4 am on the 3rd inst 1 officer & 30 men left camp to be attached to the 9nd Infantry Brigade to assist them in their numerous posts. The same evening orders were received that the Battalion would be ready to move, in fighting order, at a moments notice. Orders were also received that Battn would convoy out relief (previously ordered & cancelled) the following afternoon. On the 4th, orders were again received that relief would not take place until the afternoon of the 5th. Major the Rev D A MORRISON (CF) joined the Battalion today, also a draft of 1 officer + 109 O/Ranks	

Vol 21

War Diary
of
1/10th Liverpool R.

1st September to 30th September 1916

WAR DIARY
or
INTELLIGENCE SUMMARY
(Erase heading not required.)

Army Form C. 2118.

Hour, Date, Place	Summary of Events and Information	Remarks and references to Appendices
	PONT REMY the next day, there entraining at 1.30 P.M & proceeding to MERICOURT. On arrival at MERICOURT, orders were received that Battalion would bivouac in a cornfield about 5 miles away - men to make shelters for themselves out of corn stacks & oilsheets. During this move, the weather was very bad & the rain only ceased on arrival at the new area on the night of the 30th, all ranks having been wet thro' for 48 hours. On the 31st the Battalion moved to BIVOUACS in front of MEAULTE near BELLEVUE FARM. During the month 8 Officers reinforcements arrived from England & 100 other ranks, who had been attached to the 5th & 9th LIVERPOOLS, since coming to this country, joined the Battalion. Casualties for month:- Killed :- 5 Officers 84 Other Ranks Wounded :- 8 " 206 " " Missing :- 5 " 27 " "	

F. N. Dew Major
Commanding 10th (Scottish) Bn the King's (L'pool Regt)

Army Form C. 2118.

WAR DIARY
or
INTELLIGENCE SUMMARY

(Erase heading not required.)

Hour, Date, Place	Summary of Events and Information	Remarks and references to Appendices
	Orders were received on the 16th that the Division would be moved down the line for a rest. Entraining at RAILHEAD, EDGE-HILL, on the night of the 19th, the Battalion proceeded to MARTAINVILLE by rail, all transport having gone by road two days previously (Aug 17th). On arrival at MARTAINVILLE at 6 am on the 20th, the Battalion received orders to march to billets at VALINES, which was to be our billeting area, with the exception of one company, which was billeted in the neighbouring village of ST. MARC. Training was carried on daily, especially Bombing & musketry, for which a special trench & a 30 yards Range was dug. Parties of officers & men were granted special leave to the seaside, for 42 hours at a time to EU & AULT. On the 27th, orders were unexpectedly received that the Division would proceed up the line again & that transport would move on the 28th. The Battalion, less transport, which had moved the day before, received orders to move to a new billeting area on the 29th proceeded to MOYENNEVILLE in the afternoon & billeted there for the night, marching on to	

WAR DIARY
INTELLIGENCE SUMMARY
(Erase heading not required.)

Army Form C. 2118.

Instructions regarding War Diaries and Intelligence Summaries are contained in F. S. Regs., Part II. and the Staff Manual respectively. Title pages will be prepared in manuscript.

Hour, Date, Place	Summary of Events and Information	Remarks and references to Appendices
	that night, owing to 6th Epools having to send up one Company to assist 1/7 L'pool's. Relief ultimately completed at 10.30 AM on the 13th. The Battalion relieved the 9th LIVERPOOLS in the front line on the night of the 13th inst, relief commencing at 2 PM + being completed at 7.30 P.M. The trenches were in very bad condition, orders were issued that all men were to be dug in 5 feet below ground by daylight. This was done. Subaltern + 1 officer + 50 of 14ths working with the men in cleaning up the trench + communication trenches. The officers of the 14th was attached to the battalion was relieved the night of the 14th by the 2nd SUFFOLKS + were heavily shelled on the way back to BIVOUACS at GREAT BEAR, having about 20 casualties. This was due to the enemy putting barrage all about the road behind. The Battalion moved to billets in MEAULTE in the afternoon of the 15th + remained there until the 19th, during which time training was carried out. Major General H.S. TEUDWINE inspected the Battalion on the afternoon of the 18th + addressed the Battalion, congratulating + thanking all ranks for the way they had behaved the last few weeks, + more especially when in action on August 9th.	

WAR DIARY

INTELLIGENCE SUMMARY

(Erase heading not required.)

Army Form C. 2118.

Hour, Date, Place	Summary of Events and Information	Remarks and references to Appendices
	occupied our original front line trench. The casualties were very heavy, especially in officers, the Battalion being brought out of action by 2 Lt G.D. MORTON, who was acting adjutant. Hostile machine gun fire proving the most disturbing stock. Orders were received that night that Battalion would be relieved by 1/5 KING'S OWN, + would proceed to LIVERPOOL + LANCASTER Trenches. Major F.W.M. DREW (2nd in command) assumed command vice Lt Col. T.R. DAVIDSON wounded, + a number of Officers + other ranks, who had been left behind to replace casualties in specialists' sections, rejoined the Battalion early in the evening from the transport lines. Relief was completed at 10.45 P.M. The Battalion remained in the support trenches all day + were relieved at 8.30 P.M by the 1/5 Battn. North Staffs arriving at Bivouacs at GREAT BEAR, about 10.30 P.M. During the 11th + 12th Battalion remained at the latter camp, refitting etc, + on the afternoon of the 12th orders were received that Battn would proceed to Reserve trenches at TALUS BOISE + relieve the 6th LIVERPOOLS that night. The relief was not completed	

Army Form C. 2118.

WAR DIARY
or
INTELLIGENCE SUMMARY
(Erase heading not required.)

Instructions regarding War Diaries and Intelligence Summaries are contained in F. S. Regs., Part II. and the Staff Manual respectively. Title pages will be prepared in manuscript.

Hour, Date, Place	Summary of Events and Information	Remarks and references to Appendices
August 1916	From the 1st to the 9th August the Battalion remained in Reserve in TALUS BOISE, occupying trenches which were originally the British front line, from which the attack started on July 1st. Fatigue parties were provided both by day + by night, for work in + behind new front line, under R.E. supervision. During this time the Artillery was active on both sides, but Battalion was very lucky, only having two men killed by shell-fire. On the 9th orders were received that Battalion would be relieved that night + would proceed to Bivouacs at GREAT BEAR, where they arrived at about midnight. During the afternoon of the 8th orders were received that the Battn. would be prepared to move at short notice, + ultimately an order was issued by Brigade that Battalion would leave the camp at 8 P.M., + would proceed to trenches in front of GUILLEMONT, where they would attack Battn. moved as ordered + ultimately reached his trench about 4 A.M. on the morning of the 9th. On the way up to the trench orders were received that the Battalion would take part in an attack on GUILLEMONT at 4.20 A.M. the Battalion attacked as ordered - two separate attacks being made, + ultimately	

War Diary
of the
4/10th Liverpool Regt
for the period
1st August to 31st August
1916.

166th Brigade.
55th Division

1/10th BATTALION

THE KING'S, LIVERPOOL REGIMENT

AUGUST 1916

WAR DIARY
or
INTELLIGENCE SUMMARY.

Army Form C. 2118.

Hour, Date, Place	Summary of Events and Information	Remarks and references to Appendices

Battn on relief moved to Billets at SIMENCOURT remaining here for one night. Orders were received on the 18th to move to SOMBRIN that day. The Battn remained there for two days proceeding on the 20th to BOUQUEMAISON, billeting there for the night & marching on to BERNAVILLE the following day, where Battn remained until 25th.

On the morning of the 24th Orders were received for all transport to move at peace to new billeting area at VILLE-SUR-ANCRE. The Battn following by train on the 25th leaving BERNAVILLE at 4.30 a.m. the Battn marched to CANDAS & there entrained for MERICOURT arriving there about 6.30 p.m. & proceeding to billets at VILLE-SUR-ANCRE.

On the 27th Orders were received to proceed to SAND PIT AREA where Battn Bivouaced relieving the 1st Battn Northumberland Fusiliers of the 9th Brigade with whom we had been associated for over 17 months before leaving 2nd Army in Jany 1916.

From the 27th to the 30th training in extended Order was carried out.

On the morning of the 30th Orders were received at 8.50 a.m. to stand by ready to move at the shortest notice & at 9-12 a.m. word came from Brigade to move at 9.30 a.m. to MANSEL COPSE & at 9-40 a.m. the Battn with 1st line transport marched off. The remainder of the day was spent at the latter place "standing by". On the morning of the 31st the Battn moved

[sideways notes:]
Commanding Officers (Suffolk) 13th K.L.R.
Lt. Col. [illegible]
Commanding the (Suffolk) 13th K.L.R.

Regt

On reaching British line Sd of MONTAUBAN It was on June 30th relieved by 18" Manchester Regt (L⁶ Pals) & S.3.7.

WAR DIARY
INTELLIGENCE SUMMARY.
(Erase heading not required.)

Army Form C. 2118.

Hour, Date, Place	Summary of Events and Information	Remarks and references to Appendices
July 1916.	From the 1st to the 11th the Battn occupied the following Trenches, RAVINE, OSIERS, & WILLOWS, during which time the Battn Scouts under 2nd Lt Hodgson carried out a good deal of Patrol work keeping the enemy well within his own wire the whole time. Several Sapheads were successfully bombed. The Battn was relieved by the 118th Am Sherwood Foresters on the 11th & proceeded to SIMENCOURT billeting there for one night. On the night of the 12/13th the Brigade took over the sector in front of AGNY VILLAGE, the Battn being in Brigade Reserve took over Billets in Village, relieving the 114th Kings Own. A considerable number of fatigue parties were cut each day under R.E. & Tunnelling Coys. On the night of the 14/15th every available man was out carrying Bombs & Smoke Candles up to the front line, where a Smoke Barrage was carried out at 3 a.m. on the 15th. The enemy trenches at the same time being subjected to an intense bombardment. The Brigade was relieved on the night of the 17/18, the 8th West Ridings relieving the Battn in AGNY.	

War Diary
of the
1/10th Liverpool Regiment,
166th Infantry Brigade,
55th (West Lancashire) Division
for the period
1st July, 1916 to 31st July, 1916.

166th Brigade.
55th Division.

1/10th BATTALION

THE KING'S LIVERPOOL REGIMENT

JULY 1 9 1 6

WAR DIARY
INTELLIGENCE SUMMARY
(Erase heading not required.)

Army Form C. 2118.

Instructions regarding War Diaries and Intelligence Summaries are contained in F. S. Regs., Part II. and the Staff Manual respectively. Title pages will be prepared in manuscript.

Hour, Date, Place	Summary of Events and Information	Remarks and references to Appendices
JUNE 1916.	From the 21st night on to the end of the month our Artillery was very active bombarding both the enemy trenches & also BLAIRVILLE WOOD, whilst on the 28th the Division carried out a series of raids on the enemy trenches under cover of gas & a smoke barrage. Each Battn's Raiding Party being specially trained for the work to be done. Unfortunately just as the gas was let off the wind changed with the result that the gas & smoke missed our objective, drifting away from the enemy rap which it was arranged this party would raid, & orders were received that our party would not go over.	Roy Cukliff Capt & Adjt for Major Commanding 10th (Scottish) Bn the King's (Liverpool Regt)

WAR DIARY or INTELLIGENCE SUMMARY

1/10 Liverpool

Hour, Date, Place	Summary of Events and Information	Remarks and references to Appendices
JUNE 1916.	For the first three days of the month the Battn was in Brigade Reserve. Company work cutting a new communication trench from the GRANGE down to the village. On June 4th Orders were received that the Battn would relieve the 1/5 King's Own that evening in WILLOWS & OSIERS, relief being completed at 8 pm. Work was carried on improving the trenches, and also a considerable quantity of wire was put out each night, the enemy during this time being very quiet. On the 11th the Battn was relieved by the 1/5 King's Own & proceeded to the Rest Camp at GOUY, three being in Divisional Reserve. Numerous fatigues were furnished for Divisional Work, training was also carried out each day. On the 19th orders were received that the Battn would take over trenches on the 20th from the 1/5 King's Own also the 1/8 Bn Liverpool R. The Battn left GOUY at 10 am on the 20th & relieved the 1/8 Bn Liverpool R in the RAVINE, relief being completed at 1/30 pm & the relief of the 1/5 King's Own in OSIERS & WILLOWS being complete at 6 pm. A good deal of reconnaisance was done, Patrols under 2nd Lts Hodgson & Buck Patrolling no mans land right up to the enemy trenches wire.	

Army Form C. 2118.

WAR DIARY
— of —
INTELLIGENCE SUMMARY
(Erase heading not required.)

Instructions regarding War Diaries and Intelligence Summaries are contained in F. S. Regs., Part II. and the Staff Manual respectively. Title pages will be prepared in manuscript.

Hour, Date, Place	Summary of Events and Information	Remarks and references to Appendices
	During the month Lt-Col J.R. Davidson attended an Investiture at Buckingham Palace being decorated by H.M. the King on the morning of the 24" with the D.S.O. In his absence Capt A.G. Davidson was in Command of the Battn. 2 subtns J.C. Blackwood & S.S. Eadie the former promoted in the press joined the Battn. during the Month in addition to 29 other Ranks from England.	Rey Arthur? Lt Capt & Adjt 1/10 D.L.I. (only 1/10) (acting) Kirklinton 1/5/14.

WAR DIARY
INTELLIGENCE SUMMARY
(Erase heading not required.)

Army Form C. 2118.

Hour, Date, Place	Summary of Events and Information	Remarks and references to Appendices
MAY 1916.	On the first May the Battn in addition to holding the WILLOWS took over the OSIERS from 1/5 Kings Own Royal Lancaster R. Headquarters moving from BELLACOURT to the SUNKEN ROAD. This only proved to be a temporary arrangement as on the 3rd the Coy in OSIERS was relieved by a company of the 1/8 Battn Lancashire Regt. and on the same day 1/10 Battn took over the GRANGE from 1/5 Lancs. Headquarters moving back to BELLACOURT. The Battn crowded WILLOWS & GRANGE from the 3rd until the 11th being relieved by the 1/5 Kings Own and moving into Divisional Reserve at GOUY. Remainder there for 8 days, during which time training was carried out. The Battn was also inspected by the G.O.C 55th Divn & G.O.C 166 Brigade on successive days. On the 19th the Battn moved up to the trenches again relieving the 1/5 Kings Own in GRANGE & WILLOWS. A considerable amount of work was done between the 19th & 27th in improving the Trenches, Shell Slits, Sentry Shelters & Dug outs being constructed in addition to the ordinary work essential to keeping the trenches in good repair. The Battn was relieved by the 1/5 Kings Own on the afternoon of the 27th moving into Brigade Reserve in BELLACOURT. A number of Fatigues were provided chiefly for R.E. & other work whilst a new C.T. from GRANGE was also commenced	17h

WAR DIARY
INTELLIGENCE SUMMARY

Army, Form C. 2118.

162

Hour, Date, Place	Summary of Events and Information	Remarks and references to Appendices
APRIL - 1916.	The Battn was relieved by the 1/5 Kings Own in OSIERS & SOUTIENS on the night of the 7th/8th and proceeded to billets at SAULTY. Two Companies remained in GROSVILLE overnight rejoining the Battn on the afternoon of the 8th. The Battn remained in Divisional Reserve until the 15th during which time training was carried out and a number of R.E. fatigues were furnished. On the night of the 15/16th the Battn relieved the 1/5 South Lancs in WILLOWS & SOUTIENS, Battn H.Qrs being in BELLACOURT. A good deal of work was carried out improving Fire Trench & Communication Trenches during the next fortnight. Two drafts, one of 54 men & the other of 242 men arrived during the month, the following Officers also arriving as Reinforcements from ENGLAND :- 2/Lieuts. R.V. Clark, R. Aitken, A.C.W. Buck, R. McRae, W.A. Menzies & J.W. Marsden, the latter being sent to 166th Brigade Trench Mortar Battery. 2nd Lt. R.W. Johnson who had received his commission in the 2nd was appointed Transport Officer. From the 1st to the 17th of the month Lt. Col. J.R. Brewis in command was on the 166 Infantry Brigade whilst Brig. Genl. Green Wilkinson was on leave during which time Capt. A.G. Brewis was in command of the Battn	

WAR DIARY
INTELLIGENCE SUMMARY

Army Form C. 2118.

(Erase heading not required.)

Hour, Date, Place	Summary of Events and Information	Remarks and references to Appendices
MARCH 1916	During the month a number of changes in personnel took place viz Lieut B. Buckworth & 2nd Lt A H Noble together with Machine Gun Section complete in transport, were transferred to the 166th Brigade Machine Gun Co., Capt A N R Gager arrived out from ENGLAND, Also a Draft of 133 men from Capt H B Montgomery was in command of Battn from the 20th to 31st of the month whilst Lt-Col J R Davidson was on leave.	

Lieut. Colonel,
9th (Scottish) Bn. the King's (L'Pool Regt.)

WAR DIARY
INTELLIGENCE SUMMARY

Army Form C. 2118.

152

Hour, Date, Place	Summary of Events and Information	Remarks and references to Appendices
MARCH 1916	The Battn remained in the Trenches until relieved by 1/5 Kings Own on the night of the 6/7th. Much work had been done improving both the Fire Trench & Communication Trenches. On relief two companies were billetted in GROSVILLE the remainder of the Battn proceeding to Billets in LAHERLIERE where they were joined by the two companies from GROSVILLE on the afternoon of the 7th. Word was received that Battn would move to SAVILY on the afternoon of the 8th & would remain there until the 14th. During this time a number of fatigues were provided for R.E. work, and training was carried out under Company Commanders. Recreation in the form of football matches, Boxing contests & concerts being arranged for the men. Orders were received that Battn would relieve the 1/5 S Lancs in WILLOWS & SOUTIENS on the night of the 14/15, which relief was duly carried out, Battn HQrs being at BELLACOURT. A considerable amount of work was necessary both in Fire Trench & in Communication Trenches, this was started on the 15th & was carried out continuously by during the tour. On the night of the 30/31st the Battn was relieved by the 1/5 S Lancs & in turn relieved the 1/5 Kings Own in the OLIERS, two companies taking over the Fire Trench and in SOUTIENS & one being Duties at GROSVILLE, Battn HQrs being in the SUNKEN ROAD	

Army Form C. 2118.

WAR DIARY
INTELLIGENCE SUMMARY.
(Erase heading not required.)

Hour, Date, Place	Summary of Events and Information	Remarks and references to Appendices
FEBRUARY 1916	On the night of the 23rd/24th the Battn relieved the 1/5th Kings own at BLAMONT & RAVINE the relieve being in a very bad state owing to a heavy downfall of snow, which condition obtained until the end of the month. On the 26th the Brigade did a night relief 9Battn moved into the OSIERS being relieved at BLAMONT & the RAVINE by 13 Battn of the 164th Brigade. On the afternoon of the 29th the enemy shelled our front line with 5.9" causing several casualties, two men being killed and one wounded, Capt Cunningham R.D. who had only come out again from ENGLAND to rejoin on the 16th was seriously wounded while digging out a man who had been buried in a machine gun emplacement on which enemy had obtained a direct hit. A number of changes in Officers took place during the month. Major C.P. Symes leaving to take over command of the 119th Bn K.L.R., 2/Lts C.H. Chisman & R.M.S. Pearsall being joined to the 12th Battn K.L.R., whilst Capt A.M. McGilchrist also rejoined the Battn from ENGLAND.	

[signature]
LIEUT. COLONEL.
COMMANDING 10TH (SCOTTISH) BN THE KING'S (L'POOL REGT)

WAR DIARY
INTELLIGENCE SUMMARY
(Erase heading not required.)

Army Form C. 2118.

Hour, Date, Place	Summary of Events and Information	Remarks and references to Appendices
FEBRUARY 1916	The Battn remained at HEUCOURT until the 4th Feby on which date a move was commenced to PROUVILLE, the journey taking three days, a night being spent at LONGPRÉ and one at PERNOIS en route. Training was continued at PROUVILLE until the 10th of the month when the whole Division moved up the line in order to take over from the French who up to this time had held the sector. The journey from PROUVILLE to the RIVIERE District occupied 3 days, halts being made at AMPLIER and BERLE A BOIS, one night being spent at each Place. On the morning of the 13th just prior to going into the trenches, the Battn were shelled whilst having Breakfast at BELLACOURT, 2 men being killed & 6 wounded. 2nd Lt C R Taylor was also wounded. The trenches taken over from the French were, BLAMONT RAVINE & OSIERS, the latter being held by 1 Coy 1/5 Essex attached to us, Battn Headqrs being in the QUARRY behind BLAMONT. These positions were occupied until the night of the 18/19 when the Battn was relieved by the 1/5 Kings Own Royal Lancasters R. Two companies remained in Brigade in QUARRY to assist 1/5 Kings Own who were then a small Battn. The remainder of the Battn went into Brigade Reserve and occupied billets in GROSVILLE, work being carried on improving Communication Trenches & also the 2nd line French.	Vol 14, 15 & 16

142